D0560785

# THE MINISTRY OF INTERCESSION

# THE
# MINISTRY OF
# INTERCESSION

*A PLEA FOR MORE PRAYER*

ANDREW MURRAY, D.D.

FLEMING H. REVELL COMPANY
OLD TAPPAN, NEW JERSEY

Originally published in Great Britain
by Marshall, Morgan and Scott

ISBN 0-8007-0207-7

*Published by Fleming H. Revell Company*
*All Rights Reserved*
*Printed in the United States of America*

TO

MY BRETHREN IN THE MINISTRY

AND

OTHER FELLOW LABOURERS IN THE GOSPEL

WHOM IT WAS MY PRIVILEGE TO MEET

IN THE CONVENTIONS AT

LANGLAAGTE, JOHANNESBURG, AND HEILBRON

DURBAN AND PIETERMARITZBURG

KING WILLIAM'S TOWN, PORT ELIZABETH

AND STELLENBOSCH

THIS VOLUME

IS AFFECTIONATELY INSCRIBED

# CONTENTS

| *Chap.* | | *page* |
|---|---|---|
| | THE MINISTRY OF INTERCESSION | 9 |
| | INTRODUCTION | 15 |
| 1 | THE LACK OF PRAYER | 21 |
| 2 | THE MINISTRATION OF THE SPIRIT AND PRAYER | 27 |
| 3 | A MODEL OF INTERCESSION | 33 |
| 4 | BECAUSE OF HIS IMPORTUNITY | 40 |
| 5 | THE LIFE THAT CAN PRAY | 47 |
| 6 | RESTRAINING PRAYER—IS IT SIN? | 54 |
| 7 | WHO SHALL DELIVER? | 60 |
| 8 | WILT THOU BE MADE WHOLE? | 67 |
| 9 | THE SECRET OF EFFECTUAL PRAYER | 74 |
| 10 | THE SPIRIT OF SUPPLICATION | 81 |
| 11 | IN THE NAME OF CHRIST | 88 |
| 12 | MY GOD WILL HEAR ME | 96 |
| 13 | PAUL A PATTERN OF PRAYER | 103 |
| 14 | GOD SEEKS INTERCESSORS | 111 |
| 15 | THE COMING REVIVAL | 117 |

|  |  | *page* |
|---|---|---|
| NOTE A | | 125 |
| NOTE B | | 126 |
| NOTE C | | 127 |
| NOTE D | | 127 |
| NOTE E | | 128 |
| NOTE F | | 130 |
| HELPS TO INTERCESSION | | 133 |

# THE MINISTRY OF INTERCESSION

THERE is no holy service
    But hath its secret bliss:
Yet, of all blessed ministries,
    Is one so dear as this?
The ministry that cannot be
    A wondering seraph's dower,
Enduing mortal weakness
    With more than angel-power;
The ministry of purest love
    Uncrossed by any fear,
That bids us meet   At the Master's feet
    And keeps us very near.

God's ministers are many,
    For this His gracious will,
Remembrancers that day and night
    This holy office fill.
While some are hushed in slumber,
    Some to fresh service wake,
And thus the saintly number
    No change or chance can break.
And thus the sacred courses
    Are evermore fulfilled,
The tide of grace   By time or place
    Is never stayed or stilled.

Oh, if our ears were opened
    To hear as angels do
The Intercession-chorus
    Arising full and true,
We should hear it soft up-welling
    In morning's pearly light;
Through evening's shadows swelling
    In grandly gathering might;
The sultry silence filling
    Of noontide's thunderous glow,

And the solemn starlight thrilling
    With ever-deepening flow.


We should hear it through the rushing
    Of the city's restless roar,
And trace its gentle gushing
    O'er ocean's crystal floor:
We should hear it far up-floating
    Beneath the Orient moon,
And catch the golden noting
    From the busy Western noon;
And pine-robed heights would echo
    As the mystic chant up-floats,
And the sunny plain   Resound again
    With the myriad-mingling notes.


Who are the blessèd ministers
    Of this world-gathering band?
All who have learnt one language,
    Through each far-parted land;
All who have learnt the story
    Of Jesu's love and grace,
And are longing for His glory
    To shine in every face.
All who have known the Father
    In Jesus Christ our Lord.
And know the might   And love the light
    Of the Spirit in the Word.


Yet there are some who see not
    Their calling high and grand,
Who seldom pass the portals,
    And never boldly stand
Before the golden altar
    On the crimson-stainèd floor,
Who wait afar and falter,
    And dare not hope for more.
Will ye not join the blessed ranks
    In their beautiful array?
Let intercession blend with thanks
    As ye minister to-day!

There are little ones among them
    Child-ministers of prayer,
White robes of intercession
    Those tiny servants wear.
First for the near and dear ones
    Is that fair ministry,
Then for the poor black children,
    So far beyond the sea.
The busy hands are folded,
    As the little heart uplifts
In simple love,  To God above,
    Its prayer for all good gifts.

There are hands too often weary
    With the business of the day,
With God-entrusted duties,
    Who are toiling while they pray.
They bear the golden vials,
    And the golden harps of praise
Through all the daily trials,
    Through all the dusty ways,
These hands, so tired, so faithful,
    With odours sweet are filled,
And in the ministry of prayer
    Are wonderfully skilled.

There are ministers unlettered,
    Not of Earth's great and wise,
Yet mighty and unfettered
    Their eagle-prayers arise.
Free of the heavenly storehouse!
    For they hold the master-key
That opens all the fulness
    Of God's great treasury.
They bring the needs of others,
    And all things are their own,
For their one grand claim  Is Jesu's name
    Before their Father's throne.

There are noble Christian workers,
    The men of faith and power,
The overcoming wrestlers
    Of many a midnight hour;

Prevailing princes with their God,
   Who will not be denied,
Who bring down showers of blessing
   To swell the rising tide.
The Prince of Darkness quaileth
   At their triumphant way,
Their fervent prayer availeth
   To sap his subtle sway.


But in this temple service
   Are sealed and set apart
Arch-priests of intercession,
   Of undivided heart.
The fulness of anointing
   On these is doubly shed,
The consecration of their God
   Is on each low-bowed head.
They bear the golden vials
   With white and trembling hand;
In quiet room  Or wakeful gloom
   These ministers must stand,—


To the Intercession-Priesthood
   Mysteriously ordained,
When the strange dark gift of suffering
   This added gift hath gained.
For the holy hands uplifted
   In suffering's longest hour
Are truly Spirit-gifted
   With intercession-power.
The Lord of Blessing fills them
   With His uncounted gold,
An unseen store,  Still more and more,
   Those trembling hands shall hold.


Not always with rejoicing
   This ministry is wrought,
For many a sigh is mingled
   With the sweet odours brought.
Yet every tear bedewing
   The faith-fed altar fire
May be its bright renewing
   To purer flame, and higher.

But when the oil of gladness
   God graciously outpours,
The heavenward blaze,  With blended praise,
   More mightily upsoars.

So the incense-cloud ascendeth
   As through calm, crystal air,
A pillar reaching unto heaven
   Of wreathèd faith and prayer.
For evermore the Angel
   Of Intercession stands
In His Divine Priesthood
   With fragrance-fillèd hands,
To wave the golden censer
   Before His Father's throne,
With Spirit-fire intenser,
   And incense all His own.

And evermore the Father
   Sends radiantly down
All-marvellous responses,
   His ministers to crown;
The incense-cloud returning
   As golden blessing-showers,
We in each drop discerning
   Some feeble prayer of ours,
Transmuted into wealth unpriced,
   By Him who giveth thus
The glory all to Jesus Christ,
   The gladness all to us!

F. R. HAVERGAL.

13

# INTRODUCTION

I HAVE been asked by a friend, who heard of this book being published, what the difference would be between it and the previous one on the same subject, *With Christ in the School of Prayer*. An answer to that question may be the best introduction I can give to the present volume.

Any acceptance the former work has had must be attributed, as far as the contents go, to the prominence given to two great truths. The one was, the certainty that prayer will be answered. There is with some an idea that to ask and expect an answer is not the highest form of prayer. Fellowship with God, apart from any request, is more than supplication. About the petition there is something of selfishness and bargaining—to worship is more than to beg. With others the thought that prayer is so often unanswered is so prominent, that they think more of the spiritual benefit derived from the exercise of prayer than the actual gifts to be obtained by it. While admitting the measure of truth in these views, when kept in their true place, *The School of Prayer* points out how our Lord continually spoke of prayer as a means of obtaining what we desire, and how He seeks in every possible way to waken in us the confident expectation of an answer. I was led to show how prayer, in which a man could enter into the mind of God, could assert the royal power of a renewed will, and bring down to earth what without prayer would not have been given, is the highest proof of his having been made in the likeness of God's Son. He is found worthy of entering into fellowship with Him, not only in adoration and worship, but in having his will actually taken up into the rule of the world, and becoming the intelligent channel through which God can fulfil His eternal purpose. The book sought to reiterate and enforce the precious truths Christ preaches so continually: the blessing of prayer is that you can ask and receive what you will: the highest exercise and the glory of prayer is that persevering importunity can prevail and obtain what God at first could not and would not give.

With this truth there was a second one that came out very strongly as we studied the Master's words. In answer to the question, But why, if the answer to prayer is so positively promised, why are there such numberless unanswered prayers? we found that Christ taught us that the answer depended upon certain conditions. He spoke of faith, of perseverance, of praying in His Name, of praying in the will of God. But all these conditions were summed up in the one central one: "*If ye abide in Me,* ask whatsoever ye will and it shall be done unto you." It became clear that the power to pray the effectual prayer of faith depended *upon the life.* It is only to a man given up to live as entirely in Christ and for Christ as the branch in the vine and for the vine, that these promises can come true. "*In that day,*" Christ said, the day of Pentecost, "ye shall ask in My Name." It is only in a life full of the Holy Spirit that the true power to ask in Christ's Name can be known. This led to the emphasising the truth that the ordinary Christian life cannot appropriate these promises. It needs a spiritual life, altogether sound and vigorous, to pray in power. The teaching naturally led to press the need of a life of entire consecration. More than one has told me how it was in the reading of the book that he first saw what the better life was that could be lived, and must be lived, if Christ's wonderful promises are to come true to us.

In regard to these two truths there is no change in the present volume. One only wishes that one could put them with such clearness and force as to help every beloved fellow-Christian to some right impression of the reality and the glory of our privilege as God's children: "Ask whatsoever ye will, and it shall be done unto you." The present volume owes its existence to the desire to enforce two truths, of which formerly I had no such impression as now.

The one is—that Christ actually meant prayer to be the great power by which His Church should do its work, and that the neglect of prayer is the great reason the Church has

**16**

not greater power over the masses in Christian and in heathen countries. In the first chapter I have stated how my convictions in regard to this have been strengthened, and what gave occasion to the writing of the book. It is meant to be, on behalf of myself and my brethren in the ministry and all God's people, a confession of shortcoming and of sin, and, at the same time, a call to believe that things can be different, and that Christ waits to fit us by His Spirit to pray as He would have us. This call, of course, brings me back to what I spoke of in connection with the former volume: that there is a life in the Spirit, a life of abiding in Christ, within our reach, in which the power of prayer—both the power to pray and the power to obtain the answer—can be realised in a measure which we could not have thought possible before. Any failure in the prayer-life, any desire or hope really to take the place Christ has prepared for us, brings us to the very root of the doctrine of grace as manifested in the Christian life. It is only by a full surrender to the life of abiding, by the yielding to the fulness of the Spirit's leading and quickening, that the prayer-life can be restored to a truly healthy state. I feel deeply how little I have been able to put this in the volume as I could wish. I have prayed and am trusting that God, who chooses the weak things, will use it for His own glory.

The second truth which I have sought to enforce is that we have far too little conception of the place that intercession, as distinguished from prayer for ourselves, ought to have in the Church and the Christian life. In intercession our King upon the throne finds His highest glory; in it we shall find our highest glory too. Through it He continues His saving work, and can do nothing without it; through it alone we can do our work, and nothing avails without it. In it He ever receives from the Father the Holy Spirit and all spiritual blessings to impart; in it we too are called to receive in ourselves the fulness of God's Spirit, with the power to impart spiritual blessing to others. The power of the Church truly to bless rests on intercession—asking and receiving heavenly gifts to carry to men. Because this is so, it is no wonder that where, owing to lack of teaching or spiritual insight, we put the trust in our own diligence and effort, to the influence of

17

the world and the flesh, and work more than we pray, the presence and power of God are not seen in our work as we would wish.

Such thoughts have led me to wonder what could be done to rouse believers to a sense of their high calling in this, and to help and train them to take part in it. And so this book differs from the former one in the attempt to open a practising school, and to invite all who have never taken systematic part in the great work of intercession to begin and give themselves to it. There are tens of thousands of workers who have known and are proving wonderfully what prayer can do. But there are tens of thousands who work with but little prayer, and as many more who do not work because they do not know how or where, who might all be won to swell the host of intercessors who are to bring down the blessings of heaven to earth. For their sakes, and the sake of all who feel the need of help, I have prepared helps and hints for a school of intercession for a month (see the Appendix). I have asked those who would join, to begin by giving at least ten minutes a day definitely to this work. It is in doing that we learn to do; it is as we take hold and begin that the help of God's Spirit will come. It is as we daily hear God's call, and at once put it into practice, that the consciousness will begin to live in us, I too am an intercessor; and that we shall feel the need of living in Christ and being full of the Spirit if we are to do this work aright. Nothing will so test and stimulate the Christian life as the honest attempt to be an intercessor. It is difficult to conceive how much we ourselves and the Church will be the gainers, if with our whole heart we accept the post of honour God is offering us. With regard to the school of intercession, I am confident that the result of the first month's course will be to awake the feeling of how little we know how to intercede. And a second and a third month may only deepen the sense of ignorance and unfitness. This will be an unspeakable blessing. The confession, "We know not how to pray as we ought," is the introduction to the experience, "The Spirit maketh intercession for us"—our sense of ignorance will lead us to depend upon the Spirit praying in us, to feel the need of living in the Spirit.

18

We have heard a great deal of systematic Bible study, and we praise God for thousands on thousands of Bible classes and Bible readings. Let all the leaders of such classes see whether they could not open prayer classes—helping their students to pray in secret, and training them to be, above everything, men of prayer. Let ministers ask what they can do in this. The faith in God's word can nowhere be so exercised and perfected as in the intercession that asks and expects and looks out for the answer. Throughout Scripture, in the life of every saint, of God's own Son, throughout the history of God's Church, God is, first of all, a prayer-hearing God. Let us try and help God's children to know their God, and encourage all God's servants to labour with the assurance: the chief and most blessed part of my work is to ask and receive from my Father what I can bring to others.

It will now easily be understood how what this book contains will be nothing but the confirmation and the call to put into practice the two great lessons of the former one. *"Ask whatsoever ye will, and it shall be done to you"; "Whatever ye ask, believe that ye have received"*: these great prayer-promises, as part of the Church's enduement of power for her work, are to be taken as literally and actually true. *"If ye abide in Me, and My words abide in you"; "In that day ye shall ask in My Name"*: these great prayer-conditions are universal and unchangeable. A life abiding in Christ and filled with the Spirit, a life entirely given up as a branch for the work of the vine, has the power to claim these promises and to pray the effectual prayer that availeth much. Lord, teach us to pray.

A.M.

19

# *1*

## THE LACK OF PRAYER

"Ye have not, because ye ask not."—JAS. 4:2.

"And He saw that there was no man, and wondered that there was no intercessor."—ISA. 59:16.

"There is none that calleth upon Thy name, that stirreth up himself to take hold of Thee."—ISA. 64:7.

AT our last Wellington Convention for the Deepening of the Spiritual Life, in April, the forenoon meetings were devoted to prayer and intercession. Great blessing was found, both in listening to what the Word teaches of their need and power, and in joining in continued united supplication. Many felt that we know too little of persevering importunate prayer, and that it is indeed one of the greatest needs of the Church.

During the past two months I have been attending a number of Conventions. At the first, a Dutch Missionary Conference at Langlaagte, Prayer had been chosen as the subject of the addresses. At the next, at Johannesburg, a brother in business gave expression to his deep conviction that the great want of the Church of our day was, more of the spirit and practice of intercession. A week later we had a Dutch Ministerial Conference in the Free State, where three days were spent, after two days' services in the congregation on the work of the Holy Spirit, in considering the relation of the Spirit to prayer. At the ministerial meetings held at most of the succeeding conventions, we were led to take up the subject, and everywhere there was the confession: We pray too little! And with this there appeared to be a fear that, with the pressure of duty and the force of habit, it was almost impossible to hope for any great change.

I cannot say what a deep impression was made upon me

by these conversations. Most of all, by the thought that there should be anything like hopelessness on the part of God's servants as to the prospect of an entire change being effected, and real deliverance found from a failure which cannot but hinder our own joy in God, and our power in His service. And I prayed God to give me words that might not only help to direct attention to the evil, but, specially, that might stir up faith, and waken the assurance that God by His Spirit will enable us to pray as we ought.

Let me begin, for the sake of those who have never had their attention directed to the matter, by stating some of the facts that prove how universal is the sense of shortcoming in this respect.

Last year there appeared a report of an address to ministers by Dr. Whyte, of Free St. George's, Edinburgh. In that he said that, as a young minister, he had thought that, of the time he had over from pastoral visitation, he ought to spend as much as possible with his books in his study. He wanted to feed his people with the very best he could prepare for them. But he had now learned that prayer was of more importance than study. He reminded his brethren of the election of deacons to take charge of the collections, that the twelve might "give themselves to prayer and the ministry of the word," and said that at times, when the deacons brought him his salary, he had to ask himself whether he had been as faithful in his engagement as the deacons had been to theirs. He felt as if it were almost too late to regain what he had lost, and urged his brethren to pray more. What a solemn confession and warning from one of the high places: We pray too little!

During the Regent Square Convention two years ago the subject came up in conversation with a well-known London minister. He urged that if so much time must be given to prayer, it would involve the neglect of the imperative calls of duty "There is the morning post, before breakfast, with ten or twelve letters which *must* be answered. Then there are committee meetings waiting, with numberless other engagements, more than enough to fill up the day. It is difficult to see how it can be done."

My answer was, in substance, that it was simply a question of whether the call of God for our time and attention was of more importance than that of man. If God was waiting to meet us, and to give us blessing and power from heaven for His work, it was a short-sighted policy to put other work in the place which God and waiting on Him should have.

At one of our ministerial meetings, the superintendent of a large district put the case thus: "I rise in the morning and have half an hour with God, in the Word and prayer, in my room before breakfast. I go out, and am occupied all day with a multiplicity of engagements. I do not think many minutes elapse without my breathing a prayer for guidance or help. After my day's work, I return in my evening devotions and speak to God of the day's work. But of the intense, definite, importunate prayer of which Scripture speaks one knows little." What, he asked, must I think of such a life?

We all know the difference between a man whose profits are just enough to maintain his family and keep up his business, and another whose income enables him to extend the business and to help others. There may be an earnest Christian life in which there is prayer enough to keep us from going back, and just maintain the position we have attained to, without much of growth in spirituality or Christlikeness. The attitude is more defensive, seeking to ward off temptation, than aggressive, reaching out after higher attainment. If there is indeed to be a going from strength to strength, with some large experience of God's power to sanctify ourselves and to bring down real blessing on others, there must be more definite and persevering prayer. The Scripture teaching about crying day and night, continuing steadfastly in prayer, watching unto prayer, being heard for his importunity, must in some degree become our experience if we are really to be intercessors.

At the very next Convention the same question was put in somewhat different form. "I am at the head of a station, with a large outlying district to care for. I see the importance of much prayer, and yet my life hardly leaves room for it. Are we to submit? Or tell us how we can attain to what we desire?" I admitted that the difficulty was universal. I recalled

23

the words of one of our most honoured South African missionaries, now gone to his rest: he had the same complaint. "In the morning at five the sick people are at the door waiting for medicine. At six the printers come, and I have to set them to work and teach them. At nine the school calls me, and till late at night I am kept busy with a large correspondence." In my answer I quoted a Dutch proverb: " 'What *is* heaviest must *weigh* heaviest,'—must have the first place. The law of God is unchangeable: as on earth, so in our traffic with heaven, we only get as we give. Unless we are willing to pay the price, and sacrifice time and attention and what appear legitimate or necessary duties, for the sake of the heavenly gifts, we need not look for a large experience of the power of the heavenly world in our work. The whole company present joined in the sad confession; it had been thought over, and mourned over, times without number; and yet, somehow, there they were, all these pressing claims, and all the ineffectual resolves to pray more, barring the way. I need not now say to what further thoughts our conversation led; the substance of them will be found in some of the later chapters in this volume.

Let me call just one more witness. In the course of my journey I met with one of the Cowley Fathers, who had just been holding Retreats for clergy of the English Church. I was interested to hear from him the line of teaching he follows. In the course of conversation he used the expression—"the distraction of business," and it came out that he found it one of the great difficulties he had to deal with in himself and others. Of himself, he said that by the vows of his Order he was bound to give himself specially to prayer. But he found it exceedingly difficult. Every day he had to be at four different points of the town he lived in; his predecessor had left him the charge of a number of committees where he was expected to do all the work; it was as if everything conspired to keep him from prayer.

All this testimony surely suffices to make clear that prayer has not the place it ought to have in our ministerial and Christian life; that the shortcoming is one of which all are willing to make confession; and that the difficulties in the way of deliverance are such as to make a return to a true and full prayer-life almost impossible. Blessed be God—"The things that are impossible with men are possible with God"! "God is able to make all grace abound toward you, that ye always having all sufficiency in all things, may abound to all good work." Do let us believe that God's call to much prayer need not be a burden and cause of continual self-condemnation. He means it to be a joy. He can make it an inspiration, giving us strength for all our work, and bringing down His power to work through us in our fellowmen. Let us not fear to admit to the full the sin that shames us, and then to face it in the name of our Mighty Redeemer. *The light that shows us our sin and condemns us for it, will show us the way out of it into the life of liberty that is well-pleasing to God.* If we allow this one matter, unfaithfulness in prayer, to convict us of the lack in our Christian life which lies at the root of it, God will use the discovery to bring us not only the power to pray that we long for, but the joy of a new and healthy life, of which prayer is the spontaneous expression.

And what is now the way by which our sense of the lack of prayer can be made the means of blessing, the entrance on a path in which the evil may be conquered? How can our intercourse with the Father, in continual prayer and intercession, become what it ought to be, if we and the world around us are to be blessed? As it appears to me, we must begin by going back to God's Word, to study what *the place is God means prayer to have* in the life of His child and His Church. A fresh sight of what prayer is *according to the will of God,* of what our prayers can be, *through the grace of God,* will free us from those feeble defective views, in regard to the absolute necessity of continual prayer, which lie at the root of our failure. As we get an insight into the reasonableness and rightness of this divine appointment, and come under the full conviction of how wonderfully it fits in with God's love and our own happiness, we shall be freed from the false impression of its being an arbitrary demand. We shall with our whole heart and soul consent to it and rejoice in it, as the one only possible way for the blessing of heaven to come to earth. All thought of task and burden, of self-effort and strain, will pass away in the blessed faith that as simple as breathing is in the healthy natural life, will praying be in the Christian life that is led and filled by the Spirit of God.

As we occupy ourselves with and accept this teaching of God's Word on prayer, we shall be led to see how our failure in the prayer-life was owing to failure in the Spirit-life. Prayer is one of the most heavenly and spiritual of the functions of the Spirit-life. How could we try or expect to fulfil it so as to please God, except as our soul is in perfect health, and our life truly possessed and moved by God's Spirit? The insight into the place God means prayer to take, and which it only can take, in a full Christian life, will show us that we have not been living the true, the abundant life, and that any thought of praying more and effectually will be vain, except as we are brought into a closer relation to our Blessed Lord Jesus. Christ is our life, Christ liveth in us, in such reality that His life of prayer on earth, and of intercession in heaven, is breathed into us in just such measure as our surrender and our faith allow and accept it. Jesus Christ is the Healer of all diseases, the Conqueror of all enemies, the Deliverer from all sin; if our failure teaches us to turn afresh to Him, and find in Him the grace He gives to pray as we ought, this humiliation may become our greatest blessing. Let us all unite in praying God that He would visit our souls and fit us for that work of intercession, which is at this moment the greatest need of the Church and the world. It is only by intercession that that power can be brought down from Heaven which will enable the Church to conquer the world. Let us stir up the slumbering gift that is lying unused, and seek to gather and train and band together as many as we can, to be God's remembrancers, and to give Him no rest till He makes His Church a joy in the earth. Nothing but intense believing prayer can meet the intense spirit of worldliness, of which complaint is everywhere made.

# 2

## THE MINISTRATION OF THE SPIRIT AND PRAYER

"If ye, being evil, know how to give good gifts to your children; how much more shall your Heavenly Father give the Holy Spirit to them that ask Him?"—LUKE 11:13.

CHRIST had just said (5:9), "Ask, and it shall be given": God's giving is inseparably connected with our asking. He applies this especially to the Holy Spirit. As surely as a father on earth gives bread to his child, so God gives the Holy Spirit to them that ask Him. The whole ministration of the Spirit is ruled by the one great law: God must give, we must ask. When the Holy Spirit was poured out at Pentecost with a flow that never ceases, it was in answer to prayer. The inflow into the believer's heart, and His outflow in the rivers of living water, ever still depend upon the law: "Ask, and it shall be given." In connection with our confession of the lack of prayer, we have said that what we need is some due apprehension of the place it occupies in God's plan of redemption: we shall perhaps nowhere see this more clearly than in the first half of the Acts of the Apostles. The story of the birth of the Church in the outpouring of the Holy Spirit, and of the first freshness of its heavenly life in the power of that Spirit, will teach us how *prayer on earth, whether as cause or effect, is the true measure of the presence of the Spirit of heaven.*

We begin with the well-known words (1. 14), "These all continued with one accord in prayer and supplication." And then there follows: "And when the day of Pentecost was fully come, they were all with one accord in one place. And they were all filled with the Holy Ghost. And the same day there were added to them about three thousand souls." The great work of redemption had been accomplished. The Holy Spirit

27

had been promised by Christ "not many days hence." He had sat down on His throne and received the Spirit from the Father. But all this was not enough. One thing more was needed: the ten days' united continued supplication of the disciples. It was intense, continued prayer that prepared the disciples' hearts, that opened the windows of heaven, that brought down the promised gift. As little as the power of the Spirit could be given without Christ sitting on the throne, *could it descend without the disciples on the footstool of the throne.* For all the ages the law is laid down here, at the birth of the Church, that whatever else may be found on earth, the power of the Spirit must be prayed down from heaven. The measure of believing, continued prayer will be the measure of the Spirit's working in the Church. Direct, definite, determined prayer is what we need.

See how this is confirmed in chapter 4. Peter and John had been brought before the Council and threatened with punishment. When they returned to their brethren, and reported what had been said to them, "all lifted up their voice to God with one accord," and prayed for boldness to speak the word. 'And when they had prayed, the place was shaken, and they were all filled with the Holy Ghost, and they spake the word of God with boldness. And the multitude of them that believed were one heart and one soul. And with great power gave the apostles witness of the resurrection of the Lord Jesus; and great grace was upon them all." It is as if the story of Pentecost is repeated a second time over, with the prayer, the shaking of the house, the filling with the Spirit, the speaking God's word with boldness and power, the great grace upon all, the manifestation of unity and love—to imprint it ineffaceably on the heart of the Church: it is prayer that lies at the root of the spiritual life and power of the Church. The measure of God's giving the Spirit is our asking. He gives as a father to him who asks as a child.

Go on to the sixth chapter. There we find that, when murmurings arose as to the neglect of the Grecian Jews in the distribution of alms, the apostles proposed the appointment of deacons to serve the tables. "We," they said, "will give ourselves to prayer and the ministry of the word." It is often said, and rightly said, that there is nothing in honest business, when it is kept in its place as entirely subordinate to the kingdom, which must ever be first, that need prevent fellowship with God. Least of all ought a work like ministering to the poor hinder the spiritual life. And yet the apostles felt it would hinder them in their giving themselves to the ministry of prayer and the word. What does this teach! That the maintenance of the spirit of prayer, such as is consistent with the claims of much work, is not enough for those who are the leaders of the Church. To keep up the communication with the King on the throne and the heavenly world clear and fresh; to draw down the power and blessing of that world, not only for the maintenance of our own spiritual life, but for those around us; continually to receive instruction and empowerment for the great work to be done—the apostles, as the ministers of the word, felt the need of being free from other duties, that they might give themselves to much prayer. James writes: "Pure religion and undefiled before God and the Father is this, To visit the fatherless and widows in their affliction." If ever any work were a sacred one, it was that of caring for these Grecian widows. And yet, even such duties might interfere with the special calling to give themselves to prayer and the ministry of the word. As on earth, so in the kingdom of heaven, there is power in the division of labour; and while some, like the deacons, had specially to care for serving the tables and ministering the alms of the Church here on earth, others had to be set free for that steadfast continuance in prayer which would uninterruptedly secure the downflow of the powers of the heavenly world. The minister of Christ is set apart to give himself as much to prayer as to the ministry of the word. In faithful obedience to this law is the secret of the Church's power and success. As before, so *after Pentecost*, the apostles were men given up to prayer.

In chapter 8, we have the intimate connection between the Pentecostal gift and prayer, from another point of view. At Samaria, Philip had preached with great blessing, and many had believed. But the Holy Ghost was, as yet, fallen on none of them. The apostles sent down Peter and John to pray for them, that they might receive the Holy Ghost. The power for such prayer was a higher gift than preaching—the work of the men who had been in closest contact with the Lord in glory, the work that was essential to the perfection of the life that preaching and baptism, faith and conversion had only begun. Surely of all the gifts of the early Church for which we should long there is none more needed than the gift of prayer—prayer that brings down the Holy Ghost on believers. This power is given to the men who say: "We will give ourselves to prayer."

In the outpouring of the Holy Spirit, in the house of Cornelius at Cæsarea, we have another testimony to the wondrous interdependence of the action of prayer and the Spirit, and another proof of what will come to a man who has given himself to prayer. Peter went up at midday to pray on the housetop. And what happened? He saw heaven opened, and there came the vision that revealed to him the cleansing of the Gentiles; with that came the message of the three men from Cornelius, a man who "prayed alway," and had heard from an angel, "Thy prayers are come up before God"; and then the voice of the Spirit was heard saying, "Go with them." It is Peter praying, to whom the will of God is revealed, to whom guidance is given as to going to Cæsarea, and who is brought into contact with a praying and prepared company of hearers. No wonder that in answer to all this prayer a blessing comes beyond all expectation, and the Holy Ghost is poured out upon the Gentiles. A much-praying minister will receive an entrance into God's will he would otherwise know nothing of; will be brought to praying people where he does not expect them; will receive blessing above all he asks or thinks. The teaching and the power of the Holy Ghost are alike unalterably linked to prayer.

Our next reference will show us faith in the power that the Church's prayer has with its glorified King, as it is found, not only in the apostles, but in the Christian community. In chapter 12 we have the story of Peter in prison on the eve of execution. The death of James had aroused the Church to a sense of real danger, and the thought of losing Peter too, wakened up all its energies. It betook itself to prayer. "Prayer was made of the Church without ceasing to God for him."

That prayer availed much; Peter was delivered. When he came to the house of Mary, he found "many gathered together praying." Stone walls and double chains, soldiers and keepers, and the iron gate, all gave way before the power from heaven that prayer brought down to his rescue. The whole power of the Roman Empire, as represented by Herod, was impotent in presence of the power the Church of the Holy Spirit wielded in prayer. They stood in such close and living communication with their Lord in heaven; they knew so well that the words, "all power is given unto Me," and "Lo I am with you alway," were absolutely true; they had such faith in His promise to hear them whatever they asked —that they prayed in the assurance that the powers of heaven could work on earth, and would work at their request and on their behalf. The Pentecostal Church believed in prayer, and practised it.

Just one more illustration of the place and the blessing of prayer among men filled with the Holy Spirit. In chapter 13 we have the names of five men at Antioch who had given themselves specially to ministering to the Lord with prayer and fasting. Their giving themselves to prayer was not in vain: as they ministered to the Lord, the Holy Spirit met them, and gave them new insight into God's plans. He called them to be fellow-workers with Himself; there was a work to which He had called Barnabas and Saul; their part and privilege would be to separate these men with renewed fasting and prayer, and to let them go, "sent forth of the Holy Ghost." God in heaven would not send forth His chosen servants without the co-operation of His Church; men on earth were to have a real partnership in the work of God. It was prayer that fitted and prepared them for this; it was to praying men the Holy Ghost gave authority to do His work and use His name. It was to prayer the Holy Ghost was given. It is still prayer that is the only secret of true Church extension, that is guided from heaven to find and send forth God-called and God-empowered men. To prayer the Holy Spirit will show the men He has selected; to prayer that sets them apart under His guidance He will give the honour of knowing that they are men, "sent forth by the Holy Ghost."

It is prayer which is the link between the King on the throne and the Church at His footstool—the human link that has its divine strength in the power of the Holy Ghost, who comes in answer to it.

As one looks back upon these chapters in the history of the Pentecostal Church, how clear the two great truths stand out: where there is much prayer there will be much of the Spirit; where there is much of the Spirit there will be ever-increasing prayer. So clear is the living connection between the two, that when the Spirit is given in answer to prayer it ever wakens more prayer to prepare for the fuller revelation and communication of His Divine power and grace. If prayer was thus the power by which the Primitive Church flourished and triumphed, it is not the one need of the Church of our days? Let us learn what ought to be counted axioms in our Church work: —

Heaven is still as full of stores of spiritual blessing as it was then.     God still delights to give the Holy Spirit to them that ask Him.     Our life and work are still as dependent on the direct impartation of Divine power as they were in Pentecostal times     Prayer is still the appointed means for drawing down these heavenly blessings in power on ourselves and those around us.     God still seeks for men and women who will, with all their other work of ministering, specially give themselves to persevering prayer.

And we—you, my reader, and I—may have the privilege of offering ourselves to God to labour in prayer, and bring down these blessings to this earth. Shall we not beseech God to make all this truth so living in us that we may not rest till it has mastered us, and our whole heart be so filled with it, that the practice of intercession shall be counted by us our highest privilege, and we find in it the sure and only measure for blessing on ourselves, on the Church, and on the world?

# 3

## A MODEL OF INTERCESSION

"And he said unto them, Which of you shall have a friend, and shall go unto him at midnight, and shall say unto him, Friend, lend me three loaves; for a friend of mine is come unto me from a journey, and I have nothing to set before him; and he from within shall answer and say, Trouble me not: I cannot rise and give thee? I say unto you, Though he will not rise and give him, because he is his friend, yet, because of his importunity, he will arise and give him as many as he needeth."—LUKE 11:5–8.

"I have set watchmen upon thy walls, O Jerusalem, which shall never hold their peace day nor night: ye that are the Lord's remembrancers, keep not silence, and give Him no rest."—ISA. 62:6, 7.

WE have seen in our previous chapter what power prayer has. It is the one power on earth that commands the power of heaven. The story of the early days of the Church is God's great object-lesson, to teach His Church what prayer can do, how it alone, but it most surely, can draw down the treasures and powers of heaven into the life of earth.

Just remember the lessons we learnt of how prayer is at once indispensable and irresistible. Did we not see how unknown and untold power and blessing is stored up for us in heaven?—how that power will make us a blessing to men, and fit us to do any work or face any danger? how it is to be sought in prayer continually and persistently? how they who have the heavenly power can pray it down upon others? how in all the intercourse of ministers and people, in all the ministrations of Christ's Church, it is the one secret of success? how it can defy all the power of the world, and fit men to conquer that world for Christ? It is the power of the heavenly life, the power of God's own Spirit, the power of Omnipotence, that waits for prayer to bring it down.

In all this prayer there was little thought of personal need or happiness. It was the desire to witness for Christ and bring Him and His salvation to others, it was the thought of God's kingdom and glory, that possessed these disciples. If we would be delivered from the sin of restraining prayer, we must enlarge our hearts for the work of intercession. The attempt to pray constantly for ourselves must be a failure; it is in intercession for others that our faith and love and perseverance will be aroused, and that power of the Spirit be found which can fit us for saving men. We are asking how we may become more faithful and successful in prayer; let us see how the Master teaches us, in the parable of the Friend at Midnight, that intercession for the needy calls forth the highest exercise of our power of believing and prevailing prayer. Intercession is the most perfect form of prayer: it is the prayer Christ ever liveth to pray on His throne. Let us learn what the elements of true intercession are.

1. Notice *the urgent need*: here intercession has its origin. The friend came at midnight—an untimely hour. He was hungry, and could not buy bread. If we are to learn to pray aright we must open eye and heart to the need around us.

We hear continually of the thousand millions of heathen and Mohammedans living in midnight darkness, perishing for lack of the bread of life. We hear of five hundred millions of nominal Christians, the great majority of them almost as ignorant and indifferent as the heathen. We see millions in the Christian Church, not ignorant or indifferent, and yet knowing little of a walk in the light of God or in the power of a life fed by bread from heaven. We have each of us our own circles—congregations, schools, friends, missions—in which the great complaint is that the light and life of God are too little known. Surely, if we believe what we profess, that God alone is able to help, that God certainly will help in answer to prayer,—all this need ought to make intercessors of us, people who give their lives to prayer for those around them.

Let us take time to consider and realise the need. Each

Christless soul going down into outer darkness, perishing of hunger, with bread enough and to spare! Thirty millions a year dying without the knowledge of Christ! Our own neighbours and friends, souls intrusted to us, dying without hope! Christians around us living a sickly, feeble, fruitless life! Surely there is need for prayer. Nothing, nothing but prayer to God for help, will avail.

2. Note *the willing love.*—The friend took his weary, hungry friend into his house, and into his heart too. He did not excuse himself by saying he had no bread: he gave himself at midnight to seek it for him. He sacrificed his night's rest, his comfort, to find the needed bread. "Love seeketh not its own." It is the very nature of love to give up and forget itself for the sake of others. It takes their needs and makes them its own, it finds its real joy in living and dying for others as Christ did.

It is the love of a mother to her prodigal son that makes her pray for him. True love to souls will become in us the spirit of intercession. It is possible to do a great deal of faithful, earnest work for our fellowmen without true love to them. Just as a lawyer or a physician, from a love of his profession and a high sense of faithfulness to duty, may interest himself most thoroughly in clients or patients without any special love to each, so servants of Christ may give themselves to their work with devotion and even self-sacrificing enthusiasm without the Christlike love to souls being strong. It is this lack of love that causes so much shortcoming in prayer. It is as love of our profession and work, delight in thoroughness and diligence, sink away in the tender compassion of Christ, that love will compel us to prayer, because we cannot rest in our work if souls are not saved. True love must pray.

3. Note *the sense of impotence.*—We often speak of the power of love. In one sense this is true; and yet the truth has its limitations, which must not be forgotten. The strongest love may be utterly impotent. A mother might be willing to give her life for her dying child, and yet not be able to save it. The friend at midnight was most willing to give his friend bread, but he had none. It was this sense of impotence, of his inability to help, that sent him a-begging: "My friend is come

35

to me, and *I have nothing* to set before him." It is this sense of impotence with God's servants that is the very strength of the life of intercession.

"I have nothing to set before them": at this consciousness takes possession of the minister or missionary, the teacher or worker, intercession will become their only hope and refuge. I may have knowledge and truth, a loving heart, and the readiness to give myself for those under my charge; but the bread of heaven I cannot give them. With all my love and zeal, "I have nothing to set before them." Blessed the man who has made that "I have nothing," the motto of his ministry. As he thinks of the judgment day and the danger of souls, as he sees what a supernatural power and life is needed to save men from sin, as he feels how utterly insufficient all he can ever do is to give them life, that "*I have nothing*" urges him to pray. Intercession appears to him, as he thinks of the midnight darkness and the hungry souls, as his only hope, the one thing in which his love can take refuge.

Let us take the lesson to heart, for a warning to all who are strong and wise to work, for the encouragement of all who are feeble. The sense of our impotence is the soul of intercession. The simplest, feeblest Christian can pray down blessing from an Almighty God.

4. Note *the faith in prayer.*—What he has not himself, another can supply. He has a rich friend near, who will be both able and willing to give the bread. He is sure that if he only asks, he will receive. This faith makes him leave his home at midnight: if he has not the bread himself to give, he can ask another.

It is this simple, confident faith that God will give, that we need: where it really exists, there will surely be no mistake about our not praying. And in God's word we have everything that can stir and strengthen such faith in us. Just as the heaven our natural eye can see is one great ocean of sunshine, with its light and heat, giving beauty and fruitfulness to earth, Scripture shows us God's true heaven, filled with all spiritual blessings,—divine light and love and life, heavenly joy and peace and power, all shining down upon us. It reveals to us God waiting, delighting to bestow these blessings *in answer to prayer*. By a thousand promises and testimonies it calls and urges us to believe that prayer will be heard, that what we cannot possibly do ourselves for those whom we want to help, *can be got by prayer*. Surely there can be no question as to our believing that prayer will be heard, that through prayer the poorest and feeblest can dispense blessings to the needy, and each of us, though poor, may yet be making many rich.

5. Note *the importunity that prevails.*—The faith of the friend met a sudden and unexpected check: the rich friend refuses to hear—"I cannot rise and give thee." How little the loving heart had counted on this disappointment; it cannot consent to accept it. The supplicant presses his threefold plea: here is my needy friend, you have abundance, I am your friend; and refuses to accept a denial. The love that opened his house at midnight, and then left it to seek help, must win.

This is the central lesson of the parable. In our intercession we may find that there is difficulty and delay with the answer. It may be as if God says, "I cannot give thee." It is not easy, against all appearances, to hold fast our confidence that He will hear, and to persevere in full assurance that we shall have what we ask. And yet this is what God looks for from us. He so highly prizes our confidence in Him, it is so essentially the highest honour the creature can render the Creator, that He will do anything to train us in the exercise of this trust in Him. Blessed the man who is not staggered by God's delay, or silence, or apparent refusal, but is strong in faith, giving glory to God. Such faith perseveres, importunately, if need be, and cannot fail to inherit the blessing.

6. Note, last, *the certainty of a rich reward.*—"I say unto you, because of his importunity, he will give him as many as he needeth." Oh that we might learn to believe in the certainty of an abundant answer. A prophet said of old: "Let not your hands be weak; *your work shall be rewarded.*" Would that all who feel it difficult to pray much, would fix their eye on the recompense of the reward, and in faith learn to count upon the Divine assurance that their prayer cannot be vain. If we will but believe in God and His faithfulness,

intercession will become to us the very first thing we take refuge in when we seek blessing for others, and the very last thing for which we cannot find time. And it will become a thing of joy and hope, because, all the time we pray, we know that we are sowing seed that will bring forth fruit an hundred-fold. Disappointment is impossible: "I say unto you, He will rise and give him as many as he needeth."

Let all lovers of souls, and all workers in the service of the gospel, take courage. Time spent in prayer will yield more than that given to work. Prayer alone gives work its worth and its success. Prayer opens the way for God Himself to do His work in us and through us. Let our chief work as God's messengers, be intercession: in it we secure the presence and power of God to go with us.

"Which of you shall have a friend at midnight, and shall say to him, Friend, lend me three loaves?" This friend is none other but our God. Do let us learn that in the darkness of midnight, at the most unlikely time, and in the greatest need, when we have to say of those we love and care for, "I have nothing to set before them," we have a rich Friend in heaven, the Everlasting God and Father, who only waits to be asked aright. Let us confess before Him our lack of prayer. Let us admit that the lack of faith, of which it is the proof, is the symptom of a life that is not spiritual, that is yet all too much under the power of self and the flesh and the world. Let us in the faith of the Lord Jesus, who spake this parable, and Himself waits to make every trait of it true in us, give ourselves to be intercessors. Let every sight of souls needing help, let every stirring of the spirit of compassion, let every sense of our own impotence to bless, let every difficulty in the way of our getting an answer, just combine to urge us to do this one thing: with importunity to cry to the God who alone can help, who, in answer to our prayer, will help. And let us, if we indeed feel that we have failed, do our utmost to train a young generation of Christians, who profit by our mistake and avoid it. Moses could not enter the land of Canaan, but there was one thing he could do: he could at God's bidding "charge Joshua, and encourage him, and strengthen him" (Deut. 3:28). If it is too late for us to

38

make good our failure, let us at least encourage those who come after us to enter into the good land, the blessed life of unceasing prayer.

The Model Intercessor is the Model Christian Worker. First to get from God, and then to give to men what we ourselves secure from day to day, is the secret of successful work. Between our Impotence and God's Omnipotence intercession is the blessed link.

# 4

## BECAUSE OF HIS IMPORTUNITY

"I say unto you, Though he will not rise and give him,
because he is his friend, yet *because of his importunity*
he will arise and give him as many. as he needeth."—
LUKE 11:8.

"And He spake a parable unto them, to the end, they
ought always to pray and not to faint.... Hear what the
unrighteous judge saith. And shall not God avenge His
own elect, which *cry to Him day and night,* and *He is
long-suffering with them?* I tell you that He will avenge
them speedily."—LUKE 18:1-8.

OUR Lord Jesus thought it of such importance that we should
know the need of perseverance and importunity in prayer,
that He spake two parables to teach us this. This is proof
sufficient that in this aspect of prayer we have at once its
greatest difficulty and its highest power. He would have us
know that in prayer all will not be easy and smooth; we must
expect difficulties, which can only be conquered by per-
sistent, determined perseverance.

In the parables our Lord represents the difficulty as
existing on the side of the persons to whom the petition
was addressed, and the importunity as needed to overcome
their reluctance to hear. In our intercourse with God the
difficulty is not on His side, but on ours. In connection with
the first parable He tells us that our Father is more willing
to give good things to those who ask Him than any earthly
father to give his child bread. In the second, He assures us
that God longs to avenge His elect speedily. The need of
urgent prayer cannot be because God must be made willing
or disposed to bless: the need lies altogether in ourselves.
But because it was not possible to find any earthly illustration

of a loving father or a willing friend from whom the needed lesson of importunity could be taught, He takes the unwilling friend and the unjust judge to encourage in us the faith, that perseverance can overcome every obstacle.

The difficulty is not in God's love or power, but in ourselves and our own incapacity to receive the blessing. And yet, because there is this difficulty with us, this lack of spiritual preparedness, there is a difficulty with God too. His wisdom His righteousness, yea His love, dare not give us what would do us harm, if we received it too soon or too easily. The sin, or the consequence of sin, that makes it impossible for God to give at once, is a barrier on God's side as well as ours; to break through this power of sin in ourselves, or those for whom we pray, is what makes the striving and the conflict of prayer such a reality. And so in all ages men have prayed, and that rightly too, under a sense that there were difficulties in the heavenly world to overcome. As they pleaded with God for the removal of the unknown obstacles, and in that persevering supplication were brought into a state of utter brokenness and helplessness, of entire resignation to Him, of union with His will, and of faith that could take hold of Him, the hindrances in themselves and in heaven were together overcome. As God conquered them, they conquered God. As God prevails over us, we prevail with God.

God has so constituted us that the clearer our insight is into the reasonableness of a demand, the more hearty will be our surrender to it. One great cause of our remissness in prayer is that there appears to be something arbitrary, or at least something incomprehensible, in the call to such continued prayer. If we could be brought to see that this apparent difficulty is a Divine necessity, and in the very nature of things the source of unspeakable blessing, we should be more ready with gladness of heart to give ourselves to continue in prayer. Let us see if we cannot understand how the difficulty that the call to importunity throws in our way is one of our greatest privileges.

I do not know whether you have ever noticed what a part difficulties play in our natural life. They call out man's powers as nothing else can. They strengthen and ennoble character.

41

We are told that one reason of the superiority of the Northern nations, like Holland and Scotland, in strength of will and purpose, over those of the sunny South, as Italy and Spain, is that the climate of the latter has been too beautiful, and the life it encourages too easy and relaxing—the difficulties the former had to contend with have been their greatest boon; how all nature has been so arranged by God that in sowing and reaping, as in seeking coal or gold, nothing is found without labour and effort. What is education but a daily developing and disciplining of the mind by new difficulties presented to the pupil to overcome? The moment a lesson has become easy, the pupil is moved on to one that is higher and more difficult. With the race and the individual, it is in the meeting and the mastering of difficulties that our highest attainments are found.

It is even so in our intercourse with God. Just imagine what the result would be if the child of God had only to kneel down and ask, and get, and go away. What unspeakable loss to the spiritual life would ensue. It is in the difficulty and delay that calls for persevering prayer, that the true blessing and blessedness of the heavenly life will be found. We there learn how little we delight in fellowship with God, and how little we have of living faith in Him. We discover how earthly and unspiritual our heart still is, how little we have of God's Holy Spirit. We there are brought to know our own weakness and unworthiness, and to yield to God's Spirit to pray in us, to take our place in Christ Jesus, and abide in Him as our only plea with the Father. There our own will and strength and goodness are crucified. There we rise in Christ to newness of life, with our whole will dependent on God and set upon His glory. Do let us begin to praise God for the need and the difficulty of importunate prayer, as one of His choicest means of grace.

Just think what our Lord Jesus owed to the difficulties in His path. In Gethsemane it was as if the Father would not hear: He prayed yet more earnestly, until "He was heard" In the way He opened up for us, He learned obedience by the things He suffered, and so was made perfect; His will was given up to God; His faith in God was proved and

strengthened; the prince of this world, with all his temptation, was overcome. This is the new and living way He consecrated for us; it is in persevering prayer we walk with and
are made partakers of His very Spirit. Prayer is one form of
crucifixion, of our fellowship with Christ's Cross of our giving
up our flesh to the death. O Christians! shall we not be
ashamed of our reluctance to sacrifice the flesh and our own
will and the world, as it is seen in our reluctance to pray
much? Shall we not learn the lesson which nature and Christ
alike teach? The difficulty of importunate prayer is our highest
privilege; the difficulties to be overcome in it bring us our
richest blessings.

In importunity there are various elements. Of these the chief
are perseverance, determination, intensity. It begins with the
refusal to at once accept a denial. It grows to the determination to persevere, to spare no time or trouble, till an answer
comes. It rises to the intensity in which the whole being is
given to God in supplication, and the boldness comes to lay
hold of God's strength. At one time it is quiet and restful;
at another passionate and bold. Now it takes time and is
patient; then again it claims at once what it desires. In whatever different shape, it always means and knows—God hears
prayer: I must be heard.

Remember the wonderful instances we have of it in the
Old Testament saints. Think of Abraham, as he pleads for
Sodom. Time after time he renews his prayer until the sixth
time he has to say, "Let not my Lord be angry." He does not
cease until he has learnt to know God's condescension in each
time consenting to his petition, until he has learnt how far
he can go, has entered into God's mind, and now rests in
God's will. And for his sake Lot was saved. "God remembered
Abraham, and delivered Lot out of the midst of the over-
throw." And shall not we, who have a redemption and
promises for the heathen which Abraham never knew, begin
to plead more with God on their behalf.

Think of Jacob, when he feared to meet Esau. The angel
of the Lord met him in the dark, and wrestled with him. And
when the angel saw that he prevailed not, he said, "Let me
go." And Jacob said, "I will not let thee go." And he blessed

43

him there. And that boldness that said, "I will not," and forced from the reluctant angel the blessing, was so pleasing in God's sight, that a new name was there given to him: "Israel, he who striveth with God, for thou hast striven with God and with men, and hast prevailed." And through all the ages God's children have understood, what Christ's two parables teach, that God holds Himself back, and seeks to get away from us, until what is of flesh and self and sloth in us is overcome and we so prevail with Him that He can and must bless us. Oh! why is it that so many of God's children have no desire for this honour—being princes of God, strivers with God, and prevailing? What our Lord taught us, "What things soever ye desire, *believe that ye have received*," is nothing but His putting of Jacob's words, "I will not let Thee go except thou bless me." This is the importunity He teaches, and we must learn: to claim and take the blessing.

Think of Moses when Israel had made the golden calf. Moses returned to the Lord and said, "Oh, this people have sinned a great sin. Yet now, if Thou wilt forgive their sin—; and if not, blot me, I pray Thee, out of Thy book which Thou hast written." That was importunity, that would rather die than not have his people given him. Then, when God had heard him, and said He would send His angel with the people, Moses came again, and would not be content until, in answer to his prayer that God Himself should go with them (33:12, 17, 18), He had said, "I will do this thing also that thou hast spoken." After that, when in answer to his prayer, "Show me Thy glory," God made His goodness pass before him, he at once again began pleading, "Let my Lord, I pray Thee, go among us." And he was there with the Lord forty days and forty nights (Ex. 34:28). Of these days he says, "I fell down before the Lord, as at the first, forty days and forty nights, I did neither eat bread, nor drink water, because of all your sin which ye sinned." As an intercessor Moses used importunity with God, and prevailed. He proves that the man who truly lives near to God, and with whom God speaks face to face, becomes partaker of that same power of intercession which there is in Him who is at God's right hand and ever lives to pray.

Think of Elijah in his prayer, first for fire, and then for rain. In the former you have the importunity that claims and receives an immediate answer. In the latter, bowing himself down to the earth, his face between his knees, his answer to the servant who had gone to look toward the sea, and come with the message, "There is nothing," was "Go again seven times." Here was the importunity of perseverance. He had told Ahab there would be rain; he knew it was coming; and yet he prayed till the seven times were fulfilled. And it is of this Elijah and this prayer we are taught, "Pray for one another. Elijah was a man of like passions with ourselves. The effectual fervent prayer of a righteous man availeth much." Will there not be some who feel constrained to cry out, "Where is the Lord God of Elijah?"—this God who draws forth such effectual prayer, and hears it so wonderfully. His name be praised: He is still the same. Let His people but believe that He still waits to be inquired of! Faith in a prayer-hearing God will make a prayer-loving Christian.

We remember the marks of the true intercessor as the parable taught us them. A sense of the need of souls; a Christ-like love in the heart; a consciousness of personal importance; faith in the power of prayer; courage to persevere in spite of refusal; and the assurance of an abundant reward;—these are the dispositions that constitute a Christian an intercessor, and call forth the power of prevailing prayer. These are the dispositions that constitute the beauty and the health of the Christian life, that fit a man for being a blessing in the world, that make him a true Christian worker, who does indeed get from God the bread of heaven to dispense to the hungry. These are the dispositions that call forth the highest, the heroic virtues of the life of faith. There is nothing to which the nobility of natural character owes so much as the spirit of enterprise and daring which in travel or war, in politics or science, battles with difficulties and conquers. No labour or expense is grudged for the sake of victory. And shall we who are Christians not be able to face the difficulties that we meet in prayer? It is as we "labour" and "strive" in prayer that the renewed will asserts its royal right to claim in the name of Christ what it will, and wields its God-given power to influence the destinies of men. Shall men of the world sacrifice ease and pleasure in their pursuits, and shall we be such cowards and sluggards as not to fight our way through to the place where we can find liberty for the captive and salvation for the perishing? Let each servant of Christ learn to know his calling. His King ever lives to pray. The Spirit of the King ever lives in us to pray. It is from heaven the blessings, which the world needs, must be called down in persevering, importunate, believing prayer. It is from heaven, in answer to prayer, the Holy Spirit will take complete possession of us to do His work through us. Let us acknowledge how vain our much work has been owing to our little prayer. Let us change our method, and let henceforth more prayer, much prayer, unceasing prayer, be the proof that we look for all to God, and that we believe that He heareth us.

# 5

## THE LIFE THAT CAN PRAY

*"If ye abide in Me, and My words abide in you,* ask whatsoever ye will, and it shall be done unto you."—JOHN 15:7.

"The supplication of a *righteous man* availeth much in its working."—JAMES 5:16.

"Beloved, if our heart condemn us not, we have boldness toward God; and whatsoever we ask, we receive of Him, *because* we keep His commandments, and do the things that are pleasing in His sight."—1 JOHN 3:21, 22.

HERE on earth the influence of one who asks a favour for others depends entirely on his character, and the relationship he bears to him with whom he is interceding. It is what he is that gives weight to what he asks. It is no otherwise with God. Our power in prayer depends upon our life. Where our life is right we shall know how to pray so as to please God, and prayer will secure the answer. The texts quoted above all point in this direction. *"If ye abide in Me,"* our Lord says, ye shall ask, and it shall be done unto you. It is the prayer of a *righteous man,* according to James, that availeth much. We receive whatsoever we ask, John says, *because* we obey and please God. All lack of power to pray aright and perseveringly, all lack of power in prayer with God, points to some lack in the Christian life. It is as we learn to live the life that pleases God, that God will give what we ask. Let us learn from our Lord Jesus, in the parable of the vine, what the healthy, vigorous life is that may ask and receive what it will. Hear His voice, "If ye abide in Me, and My words abide in you, ye shall ask what ye will, and it shall be done

47

unto you." And again at the close of the parable: "Ye did not choose Me, but I chose you, and appointed you, that you should go and bear fruit, and that your fruit should abide: that *whatsoever ye shall ask* the Father in My name, *He may give it you.*"

And what is now, according to the parable, the life that one must lead to bear fruit, and then ask and receive what we will? What is it we are to be or do, that will enable us to pray as we should, and to receive what we ask? The answer is in one word: it is the branch life that gives power for prayer. We are branches of Christ, the Living Vine. We must simply live like branches, and abide in Christ, then we shall ask what we will, and it shall be done unto us.

We all know what a branch is, and what its essential characteristic. It is simply a growth of the vine, produced by it and appointed to bear fruit. It has only one reason of existence; it is there at the bidding of the vine, that through it the vine may bear and ripen its precious fruit. Just as the vine only and solely and wholly lives to produce the sap that makes the grape, so the branch has no other aim and object but this alone, to receive that sap and bear the grape. Its only work is to serve the vine, that through it the vine may do its work.

And the believer, the branch of Christ the Heavenly Vine, is it to be understood that he is as literally, as exclusively, to live only that Christ may bear fruit through him? Is it meant that a true Christian as a branch is to be just as absorbed in and devoted to the work of bearing fruit to the glory of God as Christ the Vine was on earth, and is now in heaven? This, and nothing less, is indeed what is meant. It is to such that the unlimited prayer promises of the parable are given. It is the branch-life, existing solely for the Vine, that will have the power to pray aright. With our life abiding in Him, and His words abiding, kept and obeyed, in our heart and life, transmuted into our very being, there will be the grace to pray aright, and the faith to receive the whatsoever we will.

Do let us connect the two things, and take them both in their simple, literal truth, and their infinite, divine grandeur.

The promises of our Lord's farewell discourse, with their wonderful six-fold repetition of the unlimited, *anything, whatsoever* (John 14:13, 14; 15:7, 16; 16:23, 24), appear to us altogether too large to be taken literally, and they are qualified down to meet our human ideas of what appears seemly. It is because we separate them from that life of absolute and unlimited devotion to Christ's service to which they were given. God's covenant is ever: Give all and take all. He that is willing to be wholly branch, and nothing but branch, who is ready to place himself absolutely at the disposal of Jesus the Vine of God, to bear His fruit through him, and to live every moment only for Him, will receive a Divine liberty to claim Christ's *whatsoever* in all its fulness, and a Divine wisdom and humility to use it aright. He will live and pray, and claim the Father's promises, even as Christ did, only for God's glory in the salvation of men. He will use his boldness in prayer only with a view to power in intercession, and getting men blessed. The unlimited devotion of the branch life to fruit-bearing, and the unlimited access to the treasures of the Vine life, are inseparable. It is the life abiding wholly in Christ that can pray the effectual prayer in the name of Christ.

Just think for a moment of the men of prayer in Scripture, and see in them what the life was that could pray in such power. We spoke of Abraham as intercessor. What gave Him such boldness? He knew that God had chosen and called him away from his home and people to walk before Him, that all nations might be blessed in him. He knew that he had obeyed, and forsaken all for God. Implicit obedience, to the very sacrifice of his son, was the law of his life. He did what God asked: he dared trust God to do what he asked. We spoke of Moses as intercessor. He too had forsaken all for God, "counting the reproach of Christ greater riches than all the treasures of Egypt." He lived at God's disposal: "as a servant he was faithful in all His house." How often it is written of him, "According to all that the Lord commanded Moses, so did he." No wonder that he was very bold: his heart was right with God: he knew God would hear him. No less true is this of Elijah, the man who stood up to plead for the Lord

God of Israel. The man who is ready to risk all for God can count upon God to do all for him.

It is as men live that they pray. It is the life that prays. It is the life that, with wholehearted devotion, gives up all for God and to God, that can claim all from God. Our God longs exceedingly to prove Himself the Faithful God and Mighty Helper of His people. He only waits for hearts wholly turned from the world to Himself, and open to receive His gifts. The man who loses all will find all; he dare ask and take it. The branch that only and truly lives abiding in Christ, the Heavenly Vine, entirely given up, like Christ, to bear fruit in the salvation of men, and has His words taken up into and abiding in its life, may and dare ask what it will —it shall be done. And where we have not yet attained to that full devotion to which our Lord had trained His disciples, and cannot equal them in their power of prayer, we may, nevertheless, take courage in remembering that, even in the lower stages of the Christian life, every new onward step in the striving after the perfect branch life, and every surrender to live for others in intercession, will be met from above by a corresponding liberty to draw nigh with greater boldness, and expect larger answers. The more we pray, and the more conscious we become of our unfitness to pray in power, the more we shall be urged and helped to press on towards the secret of power in prayer—a life abiding in Christ entirely at His disposal.

And if any are asking, with somewhat of a despair of attainment, what the reason may be of the failure in this blessed branch life, so simple and yet so mighty, and how they can come to it, let me point them to one of the most precious lessons of the parable of the Vine. It is one that is all too little noticed. Jesus spake, "I am the true Vine, *and my Father is the Husbandman.*" We have not only Himself, the glorified Son of God, in His divine fulness, out of whose fulness of life and grace we can draw,—this is very wonderful,—but there is something more blessed still. We have the Father, as the Husbandman, watching over our abiding in the Vine, over our growth and fruitbearing. It is not left to our faith or our faithfulness to maintain our union with Christ:

the God, who is the Father of Christ, and who united us with Him,—God Himself will see to it that the branch is what it should be, will enable us to bring forth just the fruit we were appointed to bear. Hear what Christ said of this, "Every branch that beareth fruit, He cleanseth it, that it may bear more fruit." More fruit is what the Father seeks; more fruit is what the Father will Himself provide. It is for this that He, as the Vinedresser, cleanses the branches.

Just think a moment what this means. It is said that of all fruitbearing plants on earth there is none that produces fruit so full of spirit, from which spirit can be so abundantly distilled, as the vine. And of all fruitbearing plants there is none that is so ready to run into wild wood, and for which pruning and cleansing are so indispensable. The one great work that a vinedresser has to do for the branch every year is to prune it. Other plants can for a time dispense with it, and yet bear fruit: the vine *must* have it. And so the one thing the branch that desires to abide in Christ and bring forth much fruit, and to be able to ask whatsoever it will, must do, is to trust in and yield itself to this Divine cleansing. What is it that the vinedresser cuts away with his pruning-knife? Nothing but the wood that the branch has produced—true, honest wood, with the true vine nature in it. This must be cut away. And why? Because it draws away the strength and life of the vine, and hinders the flow of the juice to the grape. The more it is cut down, the less wood there is in the branch, the more all the sap can go to the grape. The wood of the branch must decrease, that the fruit for the vine may increase; in obedience to the law of all nature, that death is the way to life, that gain comes through sacrifice, the rich and luxuriant growth of wood must be cut off and cast away, that the life more abundant may be seen in the cluster.

Even so, child of God, branch of the Heavenly Vine, there is in thee that which appears perfectly innocent and legitimate, and which yet so draws out thy interest and thy strength that it must be pruned and cleansed away. We saw what power in prayer men like Abraham and Moses and Elijah had, and we know what fruit they bore. But we also know what it cost them; how God had to separate them from their surroundings, and ever again to draw them from any trust in themselves, to seek their life in Him alone. It is only as our own will, and strength and effort and pleasure, even where these appear perfectly natural and sinless, are cut down, so that the whole energies of our being are free and open to receive the sap of the Heavenly Vine, the Holy Spirit, that we shall bear much fruit. It is in the surrender of what nature holds fast, it is in the full and willing submission to God's holy pruning-knife, that we shall come to what Christ chose and appointed us for—to bear fruit, that whatsoever we ask the Father in Christ's name, He may give to us.

What the pruning-knife is, Christ tells us in the next verse. "Ye are *clean through the word* which I have spoken to you." As He says later, "Sanctify them through Thy truth; Thy word is truth." "The word of God is sharper than any two-edged sword, piercing even to the dividing of soul and spirit." What heart-searching words Christ had spoken to His disciples on love and humility, on being the least, and, like Himself, the servant of all, on denying self, and taking the cross, and losing the life. Through His word the Father had cleansed them, cut away all confidence in themselves or the world, and prepared them for the inflowing and filling of the Spirit of the Heavenly Vine. It is not we who can cleanse ourselves: God is the Vinedresser: we may confidently intrust ourselves to His care.

Beloved brethren,—ministers, missionaries, teachers, workers, believers old and young,—are you mourning your lack of prayer, and, as a consequence, your lack of power in prayer? Oh! come and listen to your beloved Lord as He tells you, "only be a branch, united to, identified with, the Heavenly Vine, and your prayers will be effectual and much availing." Are you mourning that just this is your trouble—you do not, cannot, live this branch-life, abiding in Him? Oh! come and listen again. "*More fruit*" is not only your desire, but the Father's too. He is the Husbandman who cleanseth the fruitful branch, that it may bear more fruit. Cast yourself upon God, to do in you what is impossible to man. Count upon a Divine cleansing, to cut down and take away all that self-confidence and self-effort, that has been the cause of your failure. The

God who gave you His beloved Son to be your Vine, who made you His branch, will He not do His work of cleansing to make you fruitful in every good work, in the work of prayer and intercession too?

Here is the life that can pray. A branch entirely given up to the Vine and its aims, with all responsiblity for its cleansing cast on the Vinedresser; a branch abiding in Christ, trusting and yielding to God for His cleansing, can bear much fruit. In the power of such a life we shall love prayer, we shall know how to pray, we shall pray, and receive whatsoever we ask.

# 6

## RESTRAINING PRAYER—IS IT SIN?

"Thou restrainest prayer before God."—Job 15:4.

"What profit should we have, if we pray unto Him?"
—Job 21:15.

"God forbid that I should sin against the Lord in ceasing to pray for you."—1 Sam. 12:23.

"Neither will I be with you any more, except ye destroy the accursed from among you."—Josh. 7:12.

Any deep quickening of the spiritual life of the Church will always be accompanied by a deeper sense of sin. This will not begin with theology; that can only give expression to what God works in the life of His people. Nor does it mean that that deeper sense of sin will only be seen in stronger expressions of self-reproach or penitence: that is sometimes found to consist with a harbouring of sin, and unbelief as to deliverance. But the true sense of the hatefulness of sin, the hatred of it, will be proved by the intensity of desire for deliverance, and the struggle to know to the very utmost what God can do in saving from it—a holy jealousy, in nothing to sin against God.

If we are to deal effectually with the lack of prayer we must look at it from this point of view and ask, Restraining prayer, is it sin? And if it be, how is it to be dealt with, to be discovered, and confessed, and cast out by man, and cleansed away by God? Jesus is a Saviour from sin. It is only as we know sin truly that we can truly know the power that saves from sin. The life that can pray effectually is the life of the cleansed branch—the life that knows deliverance from the power of self. To see that our prayer-sins are indeed sins, is the first step to a true and Divine deliverance from them.

54

In the story of Achan we have one of the strongest proofs in Scripture that it is sin that robs God's people of His blessing, and that God will not tolerate it; and at the same time the clearest indication of the principles under which God deals with it, and removes it. Let us see in the light of the story if we can learn how to look at the sin of prayerlessness, and at the sinfulness that lies at the root of it. The words I have quoted above, "Neither will I be with you any more, except ye put away the accursed thing from among you," take us into the very heart of the story, and suggest a series of the most precious lessons around the truth they express, that the presence of sin makes the presence of God impossible.

1. *The presence of God is the great privilege of God's people, and their only power against the enemy.*—God had promised to Moses, *I will bring you in* unto the land. Moses proved that he understood this when God, after the sin of the golden calf, spoke of withdrawing His presence and sending an angel. He refused to accept anything less than God's presence. "For whereby shall it be known that I and Thy people have found grace in Thy sight? Is it not that *Thou goest with us*?" It was this gave Caleb and Joshua their confidence: The Lord is with us. It was this gave Israel their victory over Jericho: the presence of God. This is throughout Scripture the great central promise: I am with thee. This marks off the whole-hearted believer from the worldling and worldly Christians around him: he lives consciously hidden in the secret of God's presence.

2. *Defeat and failure are always owing to the loss of God's presence.*—It was thus at Ai. God had brought His people into Canaan with the promise to give them the land. When the defeat at Ai took place Joshua felt at once that the cause must be in the withdrawal of God's power. He had not fought for them. His presence had been withheld.

In the Christian life and the work of the Church, defeat is ever a sign of the loss of God's presence. If we apply this to our failure in the prayer-life, and as a result of that to our failure in work for God, we are led to see that all is simply owing to our not standing in clear and full fellow-

55

ship with God. His nearness, His immediate presence, has not been the chief thing sought after and trusted in. He could not work in us as He would. Loss of blessing and power is ever caused by the loss of God's presence.

3. *The loss of God's presence is always owing to some hidden sin.*—Just as pain is ordered in nature to warn of some hidden evil in the system, defeat is God's voice telling us there is something wrong. He has given Himself so wholly to His people, He delights so in being with them, and would so fain reveal in them His love and power, that He never withdraws Himself unless they compel Him by sin.

Throughout the Church there is a complaint of defeat. The Church has so little power over the masses, or the educated classes. Powerful conversions are comparatively rare. The fewness of holy, consecrated, spiritual Christians, devoted to the service of God and their fellowmen, is felt everywhere. The power of the Church for the preaching of the gospel to the heathen is paralysed by the scarcity of money and men; and all owing to the lack of the effectual prayer which brings the Holy Spirit in power, first on ministers and believers, then on missionaries and the heathen. Can we deny it that the lack of prayer is the sin on account of which God's presence and power are not more manifestly seen among us?

4. *God Himself will discover the hidden sin.*—We may think we know what the sin is: it is only God who can discover its real deep meaning. When He spoke to Joshua, before naming the sin of Achan, God first said, "They have transgressed My covenant which I commanded them." God had commanded (6:17) that all the booty of Jericho, gold and silver and all that was in it, was to be a devoted thing, consecrated unto the Lord, and to come into His treasury. And Israel had broken this consecration vow: it had not given God His due; it had robbed God.

It is this we need: God must discover to us how the lack of prayer is the indication of unfaithfulness to our consecration vow, that God should have all our heart and life. We must see that this restraining prayer, with the excuses we make for it, is greater sin than we have thought; for what does it mean? That we have little taste or relish for fellowship with

God; that our faith rests more on our own work and efforts than on the power of God; that we have little sense of the heavenly blessing God waits to shower down; that we are not ready to sacrifice the ease and confidence of the flesh for persevering waiting on God; that the spirituality of our life, and our abiding in Christ, is altogether too feeble to make us prevail in prayer. When the pressure of work for Christ is allowed to be the excuse for our not finding time to seek and secure His own presence and power in it, as our chief need, it surely proves that there is no right sense of our absolute dependence upon God; no deep apprehension of the Divine and supernatural work of God in which we are only His instruments, no true entrance into the heavenly, altogether other-worldly, character of our mission and aims, no full surrender to and delight in Christ Jesus Himself.

If we were to yield to God's Spirit to show us that all this is in very deed the meaning of remissness in prayer, and of our allowing other things to crowd it out, all our excuses would fall away, and we should fall down and cry, "We have sinned! we have sinned!" Samuel once said, "As for me, God forbid that I should sin against the Lord in ceasing to pray for you." Ceasing from prayer is sin against God. May God discover this to us. (Note A.)

5. *When God discovers sin, it must be confessed and cast out.*—When the defeat at Ai came, Joshua and Israel were ignorant of the cause. God dealt with Israel as a nation, as one body, and the sin of one member was visited on all. Israel as a whole was ignorant of the sin, and yet suffered for it. The Church may be ignorant of the greatness of this sin of restraining prayer, individual ministers or believers may never have looked upon it as actual transgression, none the less does it bring its punishment. But when the sin is no more hidden, when the Holy Spirit begins to convince of it, then comes the time of heart-searching. In our story the combination of individual and united responsibility is very solemn. The individual: as we find it in the expression, "man for man"; each man felt himself under the eye of God, to be dealt with. And when Achan had been taken, he had to make confession. The united: as we see it in all Israel first suffering and dealt with

by God, then taking Achan, and his family, and the accursed thing, and destroying them out of their midst.

If we have reason to think this is the sin that is in the camp, let us begin with personal and united confession. And then let us come before God to put away and destroy the sin. Here stands at the very threshold of Israel's history in Canaan the heap of stones in the valley of Achor, to tell us that God cannot bear sin, that God will not dwell with sin, and that if *we really want God's presence in power, sin must be put away*. Let us look the solemn fact in the face. There may be other sins, but here is certainly one that causes the loss of God's presence—we do not pray as Christ and Scripture teach us. Let us bring it out before God, and give up this sin to the death. Let us yield ourselves to God to obey His voice. Let no fear of past failure, let no threatening array of temptations, or duties, or excuses, keep us back. It is a simple question of obedience. Are we going to give up ourselves to God and His Spirit to live a life in prayer, well-pleasing to Him? Surely, if it is God who has been withholding His presence, who has been discovering the sin, who is calling for its destruction, and a return to obedience, surely we can count upon His grace to accept and strengthen for the life He asks of us. It is not a question of what you can do; it is the question of whether you now, with your whole heart, turn to give God His due, and give yourself to let His will and grace have their way with you.

6. *With sin cast out God's presence is restored.*—From this day onwards there is not a word in Joshua of defeat in battle. The story shows them going on from victory to victory. God's presence secured gives power to overcome every enemy.

This truth is so simple that the very ease with which we acquiesce in it robs it of its power. Let us pause and think what it implies. God's presence restored means victory secured. Then, we are responsible for defeat. Then, there must be sin somewhere causing it. Then, we ought at once to find out and put away the sin. We may confidently expect God's presence the moment the sin is put away. Surely each one is under the solemn obligation to search his life and see what part he may have in this evil.

God never speaks to His people of sin except with a view to saving them from it. *The same light that shows the sin will show the way out of it.* The same power that breaks down and condemns will, if humbly yielded to and waited on in confession and faith, give the power to rise up and conquer. It is GOD who is speaking to His Church and to us about this sin: "HE WONDERED that there was no intercessor." "I WONDERED that there was none to uphold." "I SOUGHT for a man that should stand in the gap before Me, and found none." The God who speaks thus is He who will work the change for His children who seek His face. He will make the valley of Achor, of trouble and shame, of sin confessed and cast out, a door of hope. Let us not fear, let us not cling to the excuses and explanations which circumstances suggest, but simply confess, "We have sinned; we are sinning; we dare not sin longer." In this matter of prayer we are sure God does not demand of us impossibilities. He does not weary us with an impracticable ideal. He asks us to pray no more than He gives grace to enable us to. He will give the grace to do what He asks, and so to pray that our intercessions shall, day by day, be a pleasure to Him and to us, a source of strength to our conscience and our work, and a channel of blessing to those for whom we labour.

God dealt personally with Joshua, with Israel, with Achan. Let each of us allow Him to deal personally with us concerning this sin, of restraining prayer, and its consequences in our life and work; concerning the deliverance from sin, its certainty and blessedness. Just bow in stillness and wait before God, until, as God, He overshadow you with His presence, lead you out of that region of argument as to human possibilities, where conviction of sin can never be deep, and full deliverance can never come. Take quiet time, and be still before God, that He may take this matter in hand. "Sit still, for He will not be in rest until He have finished this thing this day." Leave yourself in God's hands.

# 7

## WHO SHALL DELIVER?

"Is there no balm in Gilead; is there no physician there? why then is not the health of the daughter of my people recovered?"—Jer. 8:22.

"Return, ye backsliding children, and I will heal your backslidings. Behold, we come unto Thee; for Thou art the Lord our God."—Jer. 3:22.

"Heal me, O Lord, and I shall be healed."—Jer. 12:14.

"O wretched man that I am! who shall deliver me out of the body of this death? I thank God through Jesus Christ our Lord. The law of the Spirit of life in Christ Jesus made me free from the law of sin and death."—Rom. 7:24, 8:2.

DURING one of our conventions a gentleman called upon me to ask advice and help. He was evidently an earnest and well-instructed Christian man. He had for some years been in most difficult surroundings, trying to witness for Christ. The result was a sense of failure and unhappiness. His complaint was that he had no relish for the Word, and that though he prayed, it was as if his heart was not in it. If he spoke to others, or gave a tract, it was under a sense of duty: the love and the joy were not present. He longed to be filled with God's Spirit, but the more he sought it, the farther off it appeared to be. What was he to think of his state, and was there any way out of it?

My answer was, that the whole matter appeared to me very simple; he was living under the law and not under grace. As long as he did so, there could be no change. He listened attentively, but could not exactly see what I meant.

I reminded him of the difference, the utter contrariety,

between law and grace. Law demands; grace bestows. Law commands, but gives no strength to obey; grace promises, and performs, does all we need to do. Law burdens, and casts down and condemns; grace comforts, and makes strong and glad. Law appeals to self, to do its utmost; grace points to Christ to do all. Law calls to effort and strain, and urges us towards a goal we never can reach; grace works in us all God's blessed will. I pointed out to him how his first step should be, instead of striving against all this failure, fully to accept of it, and the lesson of his own impotence, as God had been seeking to teach it him, and, with this confession, to sink down before God in utter helplessness. There would be the place where he would learn that, unless grace gave him deliverance and strength, he never could do better than he had done, and that grace would indeed work all for him. He must come out from under law and self and effort, and take his place under grace, allowing God to do all.

In later conversations he told me the diagnosis of the disease had been correct. He admitted grace must do all. And yet, so deep was the thought that we must do something, that we must at least bring our faithfulness to secure the work of grace, he feared that his life would not be very different; he would not be equal to the strain of new difficulties into which he was now going. There was, amid all the intense earnestness, an undertone of despair; he could not live as he knew he ought to. I have already said, in the opening chapter, that in some of our meetings I had noticed this tone of hopelessness. And no minister who has come into close contact with souls seeking to live wholly for God, to "walk worthy of the Lord unto all well pleasing," but knows that this renders true progress impossible. To speak specially of the lack of prayer, and the desire of living a fuller prayer-life, how many are the difficulties to be met! We have so often resolved to pray more and better, and have failed. We have not the strength of will some have, with one resolve to turn round and change our habits. The press of duty is as great as ever it was; it is so difficult to find time for more prayer; real enjoyment in prayer, which would enable us to persevere, is what we do not feel; we do not possess the power to supplicate and to plead, as we should; our prayers, instead of being a joy and a strength, are a source of continual self-condemnation and doubt. We have at times mourned and confessed and resolved; but, to tell the honest truth, we do not expect, for we do not see the way to, any great change.

It is evident that as long as this spirit prevails, there can be very little prospect of improvement. Discouragement must bring defeat. One of the first objects of a physician is ever to waken hope; without this he knows his medicines will often profit little. No teaching from God's Word as to the duty, the urgent need, the blessed privilege of more prayer, of effectual prayer, will avail, while the secret whisper is heard: There is no hope. Our first care must be to find out the hidden cause of the failure and despair, and then to show how divinely sure deliverance is. We must, unless we are to rest content with our state, listen to and join in the question, "Is there no balm in Gilead; is there no physician there? why then is not the health of the daughter of my people restored?" We must listen, and receive into our heart, the Divine promise with the response it met with: "Return, ye backsliding children, and I will heal your backslidings. Behold, we come unto Thee, for Thou art the Lord our God." We must come with the personal prayer, and the faith that there will be a personal answer. Shall we not even now begin to claim it in regard to the lack of prayer, and believe that God will help us: "Heal me, O Lord, and I shall be healed."

It is always of consequence to distinguish between the symptoms of a disease and the disease itself. Feebleness and failure in prayer is a sign of feebleness in the spiritual life. If a patient were to ask a physician to give him something to stimulate his feeble pulse, he would be told that this would do him little good. The pulse is the index of the state of the heart and the whole system: the physician strives to have health restored. What everyone who would fain pray more faithfully and effectually must learn is this, that his whole spiritual life is in a sickly state, and needs restoration. It is as he comes to look, not only at his shortcomings in prayer, but at the lack in the life of faith, of which this is the symptom, that he will become fully alive to the serious nature of the disease. He will then see the need of a radical change in his whole life and walk, if his prayer-life, which is simply the pulse of the spiritual system, is to indicate health and vigour. God has so created us that the exercise of every healthy function causes joy. Prayer is meant to be as simple and natural as breathing or working to a healthy man. The reluctance we feel, and the failure we confess, are God's own voice calling us to acknowledge our disease, and to come to Him for the healing He has promised.

And what is now the disease of which the lack of prayer is the symptom? We cannot find a better answer than is pointed out in the words, "Ye are not under the law, but under grace."

Here we have suggested the possibility of two types of Christian life. There may be a life partly under the law and partly under grace; or, a life entirely under grace, in the full liberty from self-effort, and the full experience of the Divine strength which it can give. A true believer may still be living partly under the law, in the power of self-effort, striving to do what he cannot accomplish. The continued failure in his Christian life to which he confesses is owing to this one thing: he trusts in himself, and tries to do his best. He does, indeed, pray and look to God for help, but still it is he in his strength, helped by God, who is to do the work. In the Epistles to the Romans, and Corinthians, and Galatians, we know how Paul tells them that they have not received the spirit of bondage again, that they are free from the law, that they are no more servants but sons; that they must beware of nothing so much as to be entangled again with the yoke of bondage. Everywhere it is the contrast between the law and grace, between the flesh, which is under the law, and the Spirit, who is the gift of grace, and through whom grace does all its work. In our days, just as in those first ages, the great danger is living under the law, and serving God in the strength of the flesh. With the great majority of Christians it appears to be the state in which they remain all their lives. Hence the lack to such a large extent of true holy living and power in prayer. They do not know that all failure can have but one cause: *Men seek to do themselves what grace alone can do in them,* what grace most certainly will do.

Many will not be prepared to admit that this is their disease, that they are not living "under grace." Impossible, they say. "From the depth of my heart," a Christian cries, "I believe and know that there is no good in me, and that I owe everything to grace alone." "I have spent my life," a minister says, "and found my glory in preaching and exalting the doctrines of free grace." "And I," a missionary answers, "how could I ever have thought of seeing the heathen saved, if my only confidence had not been in the message I brought, and the power I trusted, of God's abounding grace." Surely you cannot say that our failures in prayer, and we sadly confess to them, are owing to our not living "under grace"? This cannot be our disease.

We know how often a man may be suffering from a disease without knowing it. What he counts a slight ailment turns out to be a dangerous complaint. Do not let us be too sure that we are not, to a large extent, still living "under the law," while considering ourselves to be living wholly "under grace." Very frequently the reason of this mistake is the limited meaning attached to the word "grace." Just as we limit God Himself, by our little or unbelieving thoughts of Him, so we limit His grace at the very moment that we are delighting in terms like the "riches of grace," "grace exceeding abundant." Has not the very term, "grace abounding," from Bunyan's book downward, been confined to the one great blessed truth of free justification with ever renewed pardon and eternal glory for the vilest of sinners, while the other equally blessed truth of "grace abounding" in sanctification is not fully known. Paul writes: "Much more shall they which receive the abundance of grace reign in life through Jesus Christ." That reigning in life, as conqueror over sin, is even here on earth. "Where sin abounded" in the heart and life, "grace did abound more exceedingly, that grace might reign through righteousness" in the whole life and being of the believer. It is of this reign of grace in the soul that Paul asks, "Shall we sin because we are under grace?" and answers, "God forbid." Grace is not only pardon of, but power over, sin; grace takes the place sin had in the life, and undertakes, as sin had reigned within in the power of death, to reign in the power of Christ's life. It is of this grace that Christ spoke, "My grace is sufficient for thee," and Paul answered, "I will glory in my weakness; for, when I am weak, then am I strong." It is of this grace, which, when we are willing to confess ourselves utterly impotent and helpless, comes in to work all in us, that Paul elsewhere teaches, "God is able to make *all grace* abound unto you, that ye, *always* having *all sufficiency* in *all things,* may abound unto *all good works."*

It has often happened that a seeker after God and salvation has read his Bible long, and yet never seen the truth of a free and full and immediate justification by faith. When once his eyes were opened, and he accepted it, he was amazed to find it everywhere. Even so many believers, who hold the doctrines of free grace as applied to pardon, have never seen its wondrous meaning as it undertakes to work our whole life in us, and *actually give us strength every moment* for whatever the Father would have us be and do. When God's light shines into our heart with this blessed truth, we know what Paul means, "Not I, but the grace of God." There again you have the twofold Christian life. The one, in which that "Not I"—I am nothing, I can do nothing—has not yet become a reality. The other, when the wondrous exchange has been made, and grace has taken the place of our effort, and we say and know, "I live, yet no longer I, but Christ liveth in me." It may then become a lifelong experience: "The grace of our Lord was exceeding abundant, with faith and love which is in Christ Jesus."

Beloved child of God! what think you, is it not possible that this has been the want in your life, the cause of your failure in prayer? You knew not how grace would enable you to pray, if once the whole life were under its power. You sought by earnest effort to conquer your reluctance or deadness in prayer, but failed. You strove by every motive of shame or love you could think of to stir yourself to it, but it would not help. Is it not worth while asking the Lord whether the message I bring you as His servant may not be more true for you than you think? Your lack of prayer is owing to a diseased state of life, and the disease is nothing but this—you have not accepted, for daily life and every duty, the full salvation which the word brings: "Ye are not under the law, but under grace." As universal and deep-reaching as the demand of the law and the reign of sin, yea, more exceeding abundant, is the provision of grace and the power by which it makes us reign in life. (Note B.)

In the chapter that follows that in which Paul wrote, "Ye are not under the law, but under grace," he gives us a picture of a believer's life under law, with the bitter experience in which it ends: "O wretched man that I am! who shall deliver me from the body of this death?" His answer to the question, "I thank God through Jesus Christ our Lord," shows that there is deliverance from a life held captive under evil habits that have been struggled against in vain. That deliverance is by the Holy Spirit giving the full experience of what the life of Christ can work in us: "The law of the Spirit of life in Christ Jesus hath made me free from the law of sin and death." The law of God could only deliver us into the power of the law of sin and death. The grace of God can bring us into, and keep us in, the liberty of the Spirit. We can be made free from the sad life under the power that led us captive, so that we did not what we would. The Spirit of life in Christ can free us from our continual failure in prayer, and enable us in this, too, to walk worthy of the Lord unto all well-pleasing.

Oh! be not hopeless, be not despondent; there is a balm in Gilead; there is a Physician there; there is healing for our sickness. What is impossible with man is possible with God. What you see no possibility of doing, grace will do. Confess the disease; trust the Physician; claim the healing; pray the prayer of faith, "Heal me, and I shall be healed." You too can become a man of prayer, and pray the effectual prayer that availeth much.[1]

---

[1] I ought to say, for the encouragement of all, that the gentle-man of whom I spoke, at a Convention a fortnight later, saw and claimed the rest of faith in trusting God for all, and a letter from England tells that he has found that His grace is sufficient.

# 8

## WILT THOU BE MADE WHOLE?

"Jesus saith unto him, Wilt thou be made whole? The impotent man answered him, Sir, I have no man to put me into the pool. Jesus saith unto him, Rise and walk. Immediately the man was made whole, and walked."—JOHN 5:6-9.

"Peter said, In the name of Jesus Christ of Nazareth, rise up and walk ... The faith which is by Him hath given this man this perfect soundness in the presence of you all."—ACTS 3:6, 16.

"Peter said, Æneas, Jesus Christ maketh thee whole: arise. And he arose immediately."—ACTS 9:34.

FEEBLENESS in prayer is the mark of disease. Impotence to walk is, in the Christian, as in the natural life, a terrible proof of some evil in the system that needs a physician. The lack of power to walk joyfully in the new and living way that leads to the Father and the throne of grace is specially grievous. Christ is the great Physician, who comes to every Bethesda where impotent folk are gathered, and speaks out His loving, searching question, Wilt thou be made whole? For all who are still clinging to their hope in the pool, or are looking for some man to put them in, who are hoping, in course of time, somehow to be helped by just continuing in the use of the ordinary means of grace, His question points to a better way. He offers them healing in a way of power they have never understood. And to all who are willing to confess, not only their own impotence, but their failure to find any man to help them, His question brings the sure and certain hope of a near deliverance. We have seen that our weakness in prayer is part of a life smitten with spiritual impotence. Let us listen to our Lord as He offers to restore our spiritual strength, to fit us for walking like healthy, strong men in all the ways of the Lord, and so be fit rightly to fill our place in the great work of intercession. As we see what the wholeness is He offers, how He gives it, and what He asks of us, we shall be prepared for giving a willing answer to His question.

## What the Health that Jesus Offers.

I might mention many marks of spiritual health. Our text leads us to take one,—walking. Jesus said to the sick man, Rise and walk, and with that restored him to his place among men in full health and vigour, able to take his part in all the work of life. It is a wonderfully suggestive picture of the restoration of spiritual health. To the healthy, walking is a pleasure; to the sick, a burden, if not an impossibility. How many Christians there are to whom, like the maimed and the halt and the lame and the impotent, movement and progress in God's way is indeed an effort and a weariness. Christ comes to say, and with the word He gives the power, Rise and walk.

Just think of this walk to which He restores and empowers us. It is a life like that of Enoch and Noah, who "walked with God." A life like that of Abraham, to whom God said, "Walk before Me," and who himself spake, "The Lord before whom I walk." A life of which David sings, "They shall walk in the light of Thy countenance," and Isaiah prophesies, 'They that wait on the Lord shall renew their strength; they shall run and not be weary, they shall walk and not faint.' Even as God the Creator fainteth not nor is weary, shall they who walk with Him, waiting on Him, never be exhausted or feeble. It is a life concerning which it could be said of the last of the Old Testament saints, Zacharias and Elisabeth, "They were both righteous before God, walking in all the commandments and ordinances of the Lord blameless." This is the walk Jesus came to make possible and true to His people in greater power than ever before.

Hear what the New Testament speaks of it: "That like as Christ was raised from the dead by the glory of the Father, so we also should walk in newness of life." It is the Risen One who says to us, Rise and walk: He gives the power of the resurrection life. It is a walk in Christ. "As ye have received Christ Jesus the Lord, so walk ye also in Him." It is a walk like Christ. "He that saith he abideth in Him ought so to walk even as He walked." It is a walk by the Spirit and after the Spirit. "Walk by the Spirit, and ye shall not fulfil the lusts of the flesh." "Who walk not after the flesh, but after the Spirit." It is a walk worthy of God and well pleasing to Him. "That ye would walk worthy of the Lord, unto all well pleasing, being fruitful in every good work." "I beseech you, that as ye received of us, how ye should walk and please God, *even as ye do walk,* that ye would abound more and more." It is a walk in heavenly love. "Walk in love, even as Christ loved you." It is a "walk in the light, as He is in the light." It is a walk of faith, all its power coming simply from God and Christ and the Holy Spirit, to the soul turned away from the world. "We walk by faith, and not by sight."

How many believers there are who regard such a walk as an impossible thing—so impossible that they do not feel it a sin that they "walk otherwise"; and so they do not long for this walk in newness of life. They have become so accustomed to the life of impotence, that the life and walk in God's strength has little attraction. But some there are with whom it is not thus. They do wonder if these words really mean what they say, and if the wonderful life each one of them speaks of is simply an unattainable ideal, or meant to be realised in flesh and blood. The more they study them, the more they feel that they are spoken as for daily life. And yet they appear too high. Oh that they would believe that God sent His Almighty Son, and His Holy Spirit, indeed to bring us and fit us for a life and walk from heaven beyond all that man could dare to think or hope for.

## How Jesus Makes Us Whole.

When a physician heals a patient, he acts on him from without, and does something which is, if possible, ever after to render him independent of his aid. He restores him to perfect health, and leaves him. With the work of our Lord Jesus it is in both respects the very opposite. Jesus works not from without, but from within, by entering Himself in the power of His Spirit into our very life. And instead of, as in the bodily healing, being rendered, if possible, independent of a physician for the future, Christ's one purpose in healing is, as we said, the exact opposite. His one condition of success, is to bring us into *such dependence upon Himself as that we shall not be able one single moment to do without Him*. Christ Jesus Himself is our life, in a sense that many Christians have no conception of. The prevailing feeble and sickly life is entirely owing to the lack of the apprehension of the Divine truth, that as long as we expect Christ continually to do something for us from heaven, in single acts of grace from time to time, and each time trust Him to give us what will last a little while, we cannot be restored to perfect health. But when once we see how there is to be nothing of our own for a single moment, and it is to be all Christ moment by moment, and learn to accept it from Him and trust Him for it, the life of Christ becomes the health of our soul. Health is nothing but life in its normal, undisturbed action. Christ gives us health by giving us Himself as our life; so He becomes our strength for our walk. Isaiah's words find their New Testament fulfilment: They that wait on the Lord shall walk and not faint, because Christ is now the strength of their life.

It is strange how believers sometimes think this life of dependence too great a strain, and a loss of our personal liberty. They admit a need of dependence, of much dependence, but with room left for our own will and energy. They do not see that even a partial dependence makes us debtors, and leaves us nothing to boast of. They forget that our relationship to God, and co-operation with Him, is not that He does the larger part and we the lesser, but that God does all and we do all—God all in us, we all through God. This dependence upon God secures our true independence; when our will seeks nothing but the Divine will, we reach a Divine nobility, the true independence of all that is created. He that has not seen this must remain a sickly Christian, letting self do part and Christ part. He that accepts the life of unceasing dependence on Christ, as life and health and strength, is made whole. As God, Christ can enter and become the life of His creature. As the Glorified One who received the Holy Spirit from the Father to bestow, He can renew the heart of the sinful creature and make it His home, and by His presence maintain it in full health and strength.

O ye all who would fain walk and please God, and in your prayer-life not have your heart condemn you, listen to Christ's words: "Wilt thou be made whole?" He can give soul-health. He can give a life that can pray, and know that it is well-pleasing to the Father. If you would have this, come and hear how you can receive it.

## WHAT CHRIST ASKS OF US.

The story invites us to notice three things very specially. Christ's question first appeals to the will, and asks for the expression of its consent. He then listens to man's confession of his utter helplessness. Then come the ready obedience to Christ's command, that rises up and walks.

1. Wilt thou be made whole? About the answer of the impotent man there could be no doubt. Who would not be willing to have his sickness removed? But, alas, in the spiritual life what need to press the question. Some will not admit that they are so sick. And some will not believe that Christ can make a man whole. And some will believe it for others, but they are sure it is not for them. At the root of all lies the fear of the self-denial and the sacrifice which will be needed. They are not willing to forsake entirely the walk after the course of this world, to give up all self-will, and self-confidence, and self-pleasing. The walk in Christ and like Christ is too straight and hard: they do not will it, they do not will to be made whole. My brother, if thou art willing, speak it out: "Lord! at any price, I will!" From Christ's side the act is one of the will: "I will, be thou clean." From your side equally: "Be it unto thee as thou wilt." If you would be delivered from your impotence—oh, fear not to say, "I will, I will!"

Then comes the second step. Christ wants us to look up to him as our only Helper. "I have no man to put me in," must be our cry. Here on earth there is no help for me. Weakness may grow into strength in the ordinary use of means, if all the organs and functions are in a sound state. Sickness needs special measures. Your soul is sick; your impotence to walk joyfully the Christian walk in God's way is a sign of disease; fear not to confess it, and to admit that there is no hope for restoration unless by an act of Christ's mercy healing you. Give up the idea of growing out of your sickly into a healthy state, of growing out from under the law into a life under grace. A few days ago I heard a student plead the cause of the Volunteer Pledge. "The pledge calls you," he said, "to a decision. Do not think of growing into a missionary: unless God forbids you, take the step; the decision will bring joy and strength, will set you free to grow up in all needed for a missionary, and will be a help to others." It is even so in the Christian life. Delay and struggle will equally hinder you; do confess that you cannot bring yourself to pray as you would, because you cannot give yourself the healthy, heavenly life that loves to pray, and that knows to count upon God's Spirit to pray in us. Come to Christ to heal you. He can in one moment make you whole. Not in the sense of working a sudden change in your feelings, or in what you are in yourself, but in the heavenly reality of coming in, in response to your surrender and faith, and taking charge of your inner life, and filling it with Himself and Spirit.

The third thing Christ asks is this, the surrender of faith. When He spoke to the impotent man His word of command had to be obeyed. The man believed that there was truth and power in Christ's word; in that faith he rose and walked. By faith he obeyed. And what Christ said to others was for him too—"Go thy way; thy faith hath made thee whole." Of us, too, Christ asks this faith, that His word changes our impotence into strength, and fits us for that walk in newness of life for which we have been quickened in Him. If we do not believe this, if we will not take courage and say, with Paul, "I can do all things in Christ, which strengtheneth me," we cannot obey. But if we will listen to the word that tells us of the walk that is not only possible, but has been proved and seen in God's saints from of old, if we will fix our eye on the mighty, living, loving Christ, who speaks in power, 'Rise and walk," we shall take courage and obey. We shall rise and begin to walk in Him and His strength. In faith, apart from and above all feeling, we shall accept and trust an unseen Christ as our strength, and go on in the strength of the Lord God. We shall know Christ as the strength of our life. We shall know, and tell, and prove that Jesus Christ hath made us whole.

Can it indeed be? Yes, it can. He has done it for many: He will do it for you. Beware of forming wrong conceptions of what must take place. When the impotent man was made whole he had still all to learn as to the use of his new-found strength. If he wanted to dig, or build, or learn a trade, he had to begin at the beginning. Do not expect at once to be a proficient in prayer or any part of the Christian life. No; but expect and be confident of this one thing, that, as you have trusted yourself to Christ to be your health and strength, He will lead and teach you. Begin to pray in a quiet sense of your ignorance and weakness, but in a joyful assurance that He will work in you what you need. Rise and walk each day in a holy confidence that He is with you and in you. Just accept Jesus Christ the Living One, and trust Him to do His work.

Will you do it? Have you done it? Even now Jesus speaks, "Rise and walk." "Amen, Lord! at Thy word I come. I rise to walk with Thee, and in Thee, and like Thee."

# 9

## THE SECRET OF EFFECTUAL PRAYER

"What things soever ye desire, when ye pray, believe
that ye have received them, and ye shall have them."—
MARK 11:24.

HERE we have a summary of the teaching of our Lord Jesus
on prayer. Nothing will so much help to convince us of the
sin of our remissness in prayer, to discover its causes, and to
give us courage to expect entire deliverance, as the careful
study and then the believing acceptance of that teaching.
The more heartily we enter into the mind of our blessed Lord,
and set ourselves simply just to think about prayer as He
thought, the more surely will His words be as living seeds.
They will grow and produce in us their fruit,—a life and
practice exactly corresponding to the Divine truth they contain. Do let us believe this: Christ, the living Word of God,
gives in His words a Divine quickening power which brings
what they say, which works in us what He asks, which actually
fits and enables for all He demands. Learn to look upon His
teaching on prayer as a definite promise of what He, by His
Holy Spirit dwelling in you, is going to work into your very
being and character.

Our Lord gives us the five marks, or essential elements,
of true prayer. There must be, first, the heart's *desire*; then
the expression of that desire in *prayer;* with that, the *faith*
that carries the prayer to God; in that faith, the *acceptance
of God's answer;* then comes *the experience* of the desired
blessing. It may help to give definiteness to our thought, if
we each take a definite request in regard to which we would
fain learn to pray believingly. Or, perhaps better still, we
might all unite and take the one thing that has been occupying our attention. We have been speaking of failure in prayer;

why should we not take as the object of desire and supplication the "grace of supplication," and say, I want to ask and receive in faith the power to pray just as, and as much as, my God expects of me? Let us meditate on our Lord's words, in the confidence that He will teach us how to pray for this blessing.

1. "What things soever *ye desire.*"—Desire is the secret power that moves the whole world of living men, and directs the course of each. And so desire is the soul of prayer, and the cause of insufficient or unsuccessful prayer is very much to be found in the lack or feebleness of desire. Some may doubt this: they are sure that they have very earnestly desired what they ask. But if they consider whether their desire has indeed been as whole-hearted as God would have it, as the heavenly worth of these blessings demands, they may come to see that it was indeed the lack of desire that was the cause of failure. What is true of God is true of each of His blessings, and is the more true the more spiritual the blessing: "Ye shall seek Me, and shall find, when ye shall search for Me with all your heart" (Jer. 29:13). Of Judah in the days of Asa it is written, "They sought Him with *their whole desire*" (2 Chron. 15:15). A Christian may often have very earnest desires for spiritual blessings. But alongside of these there are other desires in his daily life occupying a large place in his interests and affections. The spiritual desires are not all-absorbing. He wonders that his prayer is not heard. It is simply that God wants the whole heart. "The Lord thy God is *one Lord,* therefore thou shalt love the Lord thy God with *all thy heart.*" The law is unchangeable: God offers Himself, gives Himself away, to the whole-hearted who give themselves wholly away to Him. He always gives us according to our heart's desire. But not as we think it, but as He sees it. If there be other desires which are more at home with us, which have our heart more than Himself and His presence, He allows these to be fulfilled, and the desires that engage us at the hour of prayer cannot be granted.

We desire the gift of intercession, grace and power to pray aright. Our hearts must be drawn away from other desires: we must give ourselves wholly to this one. We must be willing to live wholly in intercession for the kingdom. By fixing our eye on the blessedness and the need of this grace, by thinking of the certainty that God will give it us, by giving ourselves up to it, for the sake of the perishing world, desire may be strengthened, and the first step taken towards the possession of the coveted blessing. Let us seek the grace of prayer, as we seek the God with whom it will link us, "with our whole desire"; we may depend upon the promise, "He will fulfil the desire of them that fear Him." Let us not fear to say to Him, "I desire it with my whole heart."

2. "What things soever ye desire when *ye pray*."—The desire of the heart must become the expression of the lips. Our Lord Jesus more than once asked those who cried to Him for mercy, "What wilt thou?" He wanted them to say what they would. To speak it out roused their whole being into action, brought them into contact with Him, and wakened their expectation. To pray is to enter into God's presence, to claim and secure His attention, to have distinct dealing with Him in regard to some request, to commit our need to His faithfulness and to leave it there: it is in so doing that we become fully conscious of what we are seeking.

There are some who often carry strong desires in their heart, without bringing them to God in the clear expression of definite and repeated prayer. There are others who go to the Word and its promises to strengthen their faith, but do not give sufficient place to that pointed asking of God which helps the soul to the assurance that the matter has been put into God's hands. Still others come in prayer with so many requests and desires, that it is difficult for themselves to say what they really expect God to do. If you would obtain from God this great gift of faithfulness in prayer and power to pray aright, begin by exercising yourself in prayer in regard to it. Say of it to yourself and to God: "Here is something I have asked, and am continuing to ask till I receive. As plain and pointed as words can make it, I am saying, 'My Father! I do desire, I do ask of Thee, and expect of Thee, the grace of prayer and intercession.'"

3. "What things soever ye desire, when ye pray, *believe*."—As it is only by faith that we can know God, or receive Jesus

Christ, or live the Christian life, so faith is the life and power of prayer. If we are to enter upon a life of intercession, in which there is to be joy and power and blessing, if we are to have our prayer for the grace of prayer answered, we must learn anew what faith is, and begin to live and pray in faith as never before.

Faith is the opposite of sight, and the two are contrary the one to the other. "We walk by faith, and not by sight." If the unseen is to get full possession of us, and heart and life and prayer are to be full of faith, there must be a withdrawal from, a denial of, the visible. The spirit that seeks to enjoy as much as possible of what is innocent or legitimate, that gives the first place to the calls and duties of daily life, is inconsistent with a strong faith and close intercourse with the spiritual world. "We *look not* at the things that are seen"— the negative side needs to be emphasised if the positive, "but at the things which are not seen," is to become natural to us. In praying, faith depends upon our living in the invisible world.

This faith has specially to do with God. The great reason of our lack of faith is our lack of knowledge of God and intercourse with Him. "Have faith in God," Jesus said when He spoke of removing mountains. It is as a soul knows God, is occupied with His power, love, and faithfulness, comes away out of self and the world, and allows the light of God to shine on it, that unbelief will become impossible. All the mysteries and difficulties connected with answers to prayer will, however little we may be able to solve them intellectually be swallowed up in the adoring assurance: "This God is our God. He will bless us. He does indeed answer prayer. And the grace to pray I am asking for He will delight to give." (Note C.)

4. "What things soever ye desire, when ye pray, believe that *ye have received,*" now as you pray.—*Faith has to accept the answer, as given by God in heaven, before it is found or felt upon earth.* This point causes difficulty, and yet it is of the very essence of believing prayer, its real secret. Try and take it in. Spiritual things can only be spiritually apprehended or appropriated. The spiritual heavenly blessing of God's

77

answer to your prayer must be spiritually recognised and accepted before you feel anything of it. It is faith does this. A soul that not only seeks an answer, but seeks first the God who gives the answer, receives the power to know that it has what it has asked of Him. If it knows that it has asked according to His will and promises, and that it has come to and found Himself to give it, it does believe that it has received. "We know that He heareth us."

There is nothing so heart-searching as this faith, *"Believe that ye have received."* As we strive to believe, and find we cannot, it leads us to discover what there is that hinders. Blessed is the man who holds nothing back, and lets nothing hold him back, but, with his eye and heart on God alone, refuses to rest till he has believed what our Lord bids him, "that he has received." Here is the place where Jacob becomes Israel, and the power of prevailing prayer is born out of human weakness and despair. Here comes in the real need for persevering and ever-importunate prayer, that will not rest, or go away, or give up, till it knows it is heard, and believes that it has received.

You pray for "the Spirit of grace and supplication"? As you ask for it in strong desire, and believe in God who hears prayer, do not be afraid to press on and believe that your life can indeed be changed, that the world with its press of duties, whether religious or not, hindering prayer, can be overcome, and that God gives you your heart's desire, grace to pray both in measure and in spirit, just as the Father would have His child do. "Believe that you have received."

5. "What things soever ye desire, when ye pray, believe that ye have received, and *ye shall have them.*"—The receiving from God in faith, the believing acceptance of the answer with the perfect, praising assurance that it has been given, is not necessarily the experience or subjective possession of the gift we have asked for. At times there may be a considerable, or even a long, interval. In other cases the believing supplicant may at once enter upon the actual enjoyment of what he has received. It is specially in the former case that we have need of faith and patience: faith to rejoice in the assurance of the answer bestowed and received, and to begin

and act upon that answer though nothing be felt; patience to wait if there be for the present no sensible proof of its presence. We can count upon it: *Ye shall have,* in actual enjoyment.

If we apply this to the prayer for the power of faithful intercession, the grace to pray earnestly and perseveringly for souls around us, let us learn to hold fast the Divine assurance that, as surely as we believe we receive, and that faith therefore, apart from all failing, may rejoice in the certainty of an answered prayer. The more we praise God for it, the sooner will the experience come. We may begin at once to pray for others, in the confidence that grace will be given us to pray more perseveringly and more believingly than we have done before. If we do not find any special enlargement or power in prayer, this must not hinder or discourage us. We have accepted, apart from feeling, a spiritual Divine gift by faith; in that faith we are to pray, nothing doubting. The Holy Spirit may for a little time be hiding Himself within us; we may count upon Him, even though it be with groanings which cannot find expression, to pray in us; in due time we shall become conscious of His presence and power. As sure as there is desire and prayer and faith, and faith's acceptance of the gift, there will be, too, the manifestation and experience of the blessing we sought.

Beloved brother! do you truly desire that God should enable you so to pray that your life may be free from continual self-condemnation, and that the power of His Spirit may come down in answer to your petition? Come and *ask it of God.* Kneel down and pray for it in a single definite sentence. When you have done so, kneel still in faith, believing in God who answers. Believe that you do now receive what you have prayed: believe that you have received. If you find it difficult to do this, kneel still, and say that you do it on the strength of His own word. If it cost time, and struggle, and doubt—fear not; at His feet, looking up into His face, faith will come. "Believe that you have received": at His bidding you dare claim the answer. Begin in that faith, even though it be feeble, a new prayer-life, with this one thought as its strength: "You have asked and received grace in Christ to prepare you, step by step, to be faithful in prayer and intercession. The more simply you hold to this, and expect the Holy Spirit to work it in you, the more surely and fully will the word be made true to you: Ye shall have it. God Himself who gave the answer will work it in you."

# *10*

## THE SPIRIT OF SUPPLICATION

"I will pour upon the house of David the Spirit of grace and of supplication."—ZECH. 12:10.

"The Spirit also helpeth our infirmity; for we know not how to pray as we ought: but the Spirit Himself maketh intercession for us with groanings which cannot be uttered. And He that searcheth the hearts knoweth what is the mind of the Spirit, because He maketh intercession for the saints according to God."—ROM. 8:26, 27.

"With all prayer and supplication praying at all seasons in the Spirit, and watching thereunto in all perseverance and supplication for all the saints."—EPH. 6:18.

"Praying in the Holy Spirit."—JUDE 20.

THE Holy Spirit has been given to every child of God to be his life. He dwells in him, not as a separate Being in one part of his nature, but as his very life. He is the Divine power or energy by which his life is maintained and strengthened. All that a believer is called to be or to do, the Holy Spirit can and will work in him. If he does not know or yield to the Holy Guest, the Blessed Spirit cannot work, and his life is a sickly one, full of failure and of sin. As he yields, and waits, and obeys the leading of the Spirit, God works in him all that is pleasing in His sight.

This Holy Spirit is, in the first place, a Spirit of prayer. He was promised as a "Spirit of grace and supplication," the grace for supplication. He was sent forth into our hearts as "the Spirit of adoption, whereby we cry, Abba, Father." He enables us to say, in true faith and growing apprehension of its meaning, Our Father which art in heaven. "He maketh intercession for the saints according to God." And as we pray in the Spirit, our worship is as God seeks it to be, "in spirit and in truth." Prayer is just the breathing of the Spirit in us; power in prayer comes from the power of the Spirit in us, waited on and trusted in. Failure in prayer comes from feebleness of the Spirit's work in us. Our prayer is the index of the measure of the Spirit's work in us. To pray aright, the life of the Spirit must be right in us. For praying the effectual, much-availing prayer of the righteous man everything depends on being full of the Spirit.

There are three very simple lessons that the believer, who would enjoy the blessing of being taught to pray by the Spirit of prayer, must know. The first is: *Believe that the Spirit dwells in you* (Eph. 1:13). Deep in the inmost recesses of his being, hidden and unfelt, every child of God has the Holy, Mighty Spirit of God dwelling in him. He knows it by faith, the faith that, accepting God's word, realises that of which he sees as yet no sign. "We receive the promise of the Spirit by faith." As long as we measure our power, for praying aright and perseveringly, by what we feel, or think we can accomplish, we shall be discouraged when we hear of how much we ought to pray. But when we quietly believe that, in the midst of all our conscious weakness, the Holy Spirit as a Spirit of supplication is dwelling within us, *for the very purpose of enabling us to pray in such manner and measure as God would have us,* our hearts will be filled with hope. We shall be strengthened in the assurance which lies at the very root of a happy and fruitful Christian life, that *God has made an abundant provision for our being what He wants us to be.* We shall begin to lose our sense of burden and fear and discouragement about our ever praying sufficiently, because we see that the Holy Spirit Himself will pray, is praying, in us.

The second lesson is: *Beware above everything of grieving the Holy Spirit* (Eph. 4:30). If you do, how can He work in you the quiet, trustful, and blessed sense of that union with Christ which makes your prayers well pleasing to the Father? Beware of grieving Him by sin, by unbelief, by selfishness, by unfaithfulness to His voice in conscience. Do not think grieving Him a necessity: that cuts away the very sinews of your strength. Do not consider it impossible to obey the command, "Grieve not the Holy Spirit." He Himself is the very power of God to make you obedient. The sin that comes up in you against your will, the tendency to sloth, or pride, or self-will, or passion that rises in the flesh, your will can, in the power of the Spirit, at once reject, and cast upon Christ and His blood, and your communion with God is immediately restored. Accept each day the Holy Spirit as your Leader and Life and Strength; you can count upon Him to do in your heart all that ought to be done there. He, the Unseen and Unfelt One, but known by faith, gives there, unseen and unfelt, the love and the faith and the power of obedience you need, because He reveals Christ unseen within you, as actually your Life and Strength. Grieve not the Holy Spirit by distrusting Him, because you do not feel His presence in you.

Especially in the matter of prayer grieve Him not. Do not expect, when you trust Christ to bring you into a new, healthy prayer-life, that you will be able all at once to pray as easily and powerfully and joyfully as you fain would. No; it may not come at once. But just how quietly before God in your ignorance and weakness. That is the best and truest prayer, to put yourself before God just as you are, and to count on the hidden Spirit praying in you. "We know not what to pray as we ought"; ignorance, difficulty, struggle, marks our prayer all along. But, "the Spirit helpeth our infirmities." How? "The Spirit Himself," deeper down than our thoughts or feelings, "maketh intercession for us with groanings which cannot be uttered." When you cannot find words, when your words appear cold and feeble, just believe: The Holy Spirit is praying in me. Be quiet before God, and give Him time and opportunity; in due season you will learn to pray. Beware of grieving the Spirit of prayer, by not honouring Him in patient, trustful surrender to His intercession in you.

The third lesson: *"Be filled with the Spirit"* (Eph. 5:18). I think that we have seen the meaning of the great truth: It is only the healthy spiritual life that can pray aright. The command comes to each of us: "Be filled with the Spirit." That implies that while some rest content with the beginning, with a small measure of the Spirit's working, it is God's will that we should be filled with the Spirit. That means, from our side, that our whole being ought to be entirely yielded up to the Holy Spirit, to be possessed and controlled by Him alone. And, from God's side, that we may count upon and expect the Holy Spirit to take possession and fill us. Has not our failure in prayer evidently been owing to our not having accepted the Spirit of prayer to be our life; to our not having yielded wholly to Him, whom the Father gave as the Spirit of His Son, to work the life of the Son in us? Let us, to say the very least, be willing to receive Him, to yield ourselves to God and trust Him for it. Let us not again wilfully grieve the Holy Spirit by declining, by neglecting, by hesitating to seek to have Him as fully as He is willing to give Himself to us. If we have at all seen that prayer is the great need of our work and of the Church, if we have at all desired or resolved to pray more, let us turn to the very source of all power and blessing—let us believe that the Spirit of prayer, even in His fulness, is for us.

We all admit the place the Father and the Son have in our prayer. It is to the Father we pray, and from whom we expect the answer. It is in the merit, and name, and life of the Son, abiding in Him and He in us, that we trust to be heard. But have we understood that in the Holy Trinity all the Three Persons have an equal place in prayer, and that the faith in the Holy Spirit of intercession as praying in us is as indispensable as the faith in the Father and the Son? How clear we have this in the words, "Through Christ we have access by one Spirit to the Father." As much as prayer must be *to* the Father, and *through* the Son, it must be *by* the Spirit. And the Spirit can pray in no other way in us, than as He lives in us. It is only as we give ourselves to the Spirit living and praying in us, that the glory of the prayer-hearing God, and the ever-blessed and most effectual mediation of the Son, can be known by us in their power. (Note D.)

Our last lesson: *Pray in the Spirit for all saints* (Eph. 6: 18). The Spirit, who is called "the Spirit of supplication," is also and very specially the Spirit of intercession. It is said of Him, "the Spirit Himself maketh intercession for us with groanings that cannot be uttered." "He maketh intercession for the saints." It is the same word as is used of Christ, "who also maketh intercession for us." The thought is essentially that of mediation—one pleading for another. When the Spirit of intercession takes full possession of us, all selfishness, as if we wanted Him separate from His intercession for others, and have Him for ourselves alone, is banished, and we begin to avail ourselves of our wonderful privilege to plead for men. We long to live the Christ-life of self-consuming sacrifice for others, as our heart unceasingly yields itself to God to obtain His blessing for those around us. Intercession then becomes, not an incident or an occasional part of our prayers, but their one great object. Prayer for ourselves then takes its true place, simply as a means for fitting us better for exercising our ministry of intercession more effectually.

May I be allowed to speak a very personal word to each of my readers? I have humbly besought God to give me what I may give them—Divine light and help truly to forsake the life of failure in prayer, and to enter, even now, and at once, upon the life of intercession which the Holy Spirit can enable them to lead. It can be done by a simple act of faith, claiming the fulness of the Spirit, that is, the full measure of the Spirit which you are capable in God's sight of receiving, and He is therefore willing to bestow. Will you not, even now, accept of this by faith?

Let me remind you of what takes place at conversion. Most of us, you probably too, for a time sought peace in efforts and struggles to give up sin and please God. But you did not find it thus. The peace of God's pardon came by faith, trusting God's word concerning Christ and His salvation. You had heard of Christ as the gift of His love, you knew that He was for you too, you had felt the movings and drawings of His grace; but never till in faith in God's word you accepted Him as God's gift to you, did you know the peace and joy that He can give. Believing in Him and His saving love made all the difference, and changed your relation from one who had ever grieved Him, to one who loved and served Him. And yet, after a time, you have a thousand times wondered you love and serve Him so ill.

At the time of your conversion you knew little about the

85

Holy Spirit. Later on you heard of His dwelling in you, and His being the power of God in you for all the Father intends you to be, and yet His indwelling and inworking have been something vague and indefinite, and hardly a source of joy or strength. At conversion you did not yet know your need of Him, and still less what you might expect of Him. But your failures have taught it you. And now you begin to see how you have been grieving Him, by not trusting and not following Him, by not allowing Him to work in you all God's pleasure.

All this can be changed. Just as you, after seeking Christ, and praying to Him, and trying without success to serve Him, found rest in accepting Him by faith, just so you may even now yield yourself to the full guidance of the Holy Spirit, and claim and accept Him to work in you what God would have. Will you not do it? Just accept Him in faith as Christ's gift, to be the Spirit of your whole life, of your prayer-life too, and you can count upon Him to take charge. You can then begin, however feeble you feel, and unable to pray aright, to bow before God in silence, with the assurance that He will teach you to pray.

My dear brother, as you consciously by faith accepted Christ, to pardon, you can consciously now in the like faith accept of Christ who gives the Holy Spirit to do His work in you. "Christ redeemed us that we might receive the promise of the Spirit by faith." Kneel down, and simply believe that the Lord Christ, who baptizeth with the Holy Spirit, does now, in response to your faith, begin in you the blessed life of a full experience of the power of the indwelling Spirit. Depend most confidently upon Him, apart from all feeling or experience, as the Spirit of supplication and intercession to do His work. Renew that act of faith each morning, each time you pray; trust Him, against all appearances, to work in you,—be sure He is working,—and He will give you to know what the joy of the Holy Spirit is as the power of your life.

"I will pour out the Spirit of supplication." Do you not begin to see that the mystery of prayer is the mystery of the Divine indwelling. God in heaven gives His Spirit in our hearts to be there the Divine power praying in us, and drawing us upward to our God. God is a Spirit, and nothing but a like life and Spirit within us can hold communion with Him. It was for this man was created, that God might dwell and work in Him, and be the life of his life. It was this Divine indwelling that sin lost. It was this that Christ came to exhibit in His life, to win back for us in His death, and then to impart to us by coming again from heaven in the Spirit to live in His disciples. It is this, the indwelling of God through the Spirit, that alone can explain and enable us to appropriate the wonderful promises given to prayer. God gives the Spirit as a Spirit of Supplication, too, to maintain His Divine life within us as a life out of which prayer ever rises upward.

Without the Holy Spirit no man can call Jesus Lord, or cry, Abba, Father; no man can worship in spirit and truth, or pray without ceasing. The Holy Spirit is given the believer to be and do in him all that God wants him to be or do. He is given him especially as the Spirit of prayer and supplication. Is it not clear that everything in prayer depends upon our trusting the Holy Spirit to do His work in us; yielding ourselves to His leading, depending only and wholly on Him?

We read, "Stephen was a man full of faith and the Holy Spirit." The two ever go together, in exact proportion to each other. As our faith sees and trusts the Spirit in us to pray, and waits on Him, He will do His work; and it is the longing desire, and the earnest supplication, and the definite faith the Father seeks. Do let us know Him, and in the faith of Christ who unceasingly gives Him, cultivate the assured confidence, we can learn to pray as the Father would have us.

# 11

## IN THE NAME OF CHRIST

"Whatsoever ye shall ask *in My Name*, that will I do. If ye shall ask anything *in My Name*, I will do it. I have appointed you, that whatsoever ye shall ask of the Father *in My Name*, He may give it you. Verily, verily I say unto you, whatsoever ye shall ask the Father *in My Name*, He will give it you. Hitherto have ye asked nothing *in My Name;* ask, and ye shall receive, that your joy may be full. At that day ye shall ask *in My Name*."
—JOHN 14:13, 14, 15:16, 16:23, 24, 26.

IN My Name—repeated six times over. Our Lord knew how slow our hearts would be to take it in, and He so longed that we should really believe that His Name is the power in which every knee should bow, and in which every prayer could be heard, that He did not weary of saying it over and over: *In My Name!* Between the wonderful *whatsoever ye shall ask,* and the Divine *I will do it, the Father will give it,* this one word is the simple link: *In My Name.* Our asking and the Father's giving are to be equally in the Name of Christ. Everything in prayer depends upon our apprehending this— *In My Name.*

We know what a name is: a word by which we call up to our mind the whole being and nature of an object. When I speak of a lamb or a lion, the name at once suggests the different nature peculiar to each. The Name of God is meant to express His whole Divine nature and glory. And so the Name of Christ means His whole nature, His person and work, His disposition and Spirit. To ask in the Name of Christ is to pray in union with Him. When first a sinner believes in Christ, he only knows and thinks of His merit and intercession. And to the very end that is the one foundation of our confidence. And yet, as the believer grows in grace and enters more deeply and truly into union with Christ—that is, as he abides in Him —he learns that to pray in the Name of Christ also means in His Spirit, and in the possession of His nature, as the Holy Spirit imparts it to us. As we grasp the meaning of the words, "*At that day* ye shall ask in My Name"—the day when in the Holy Spirit Christ came to live in His disciples—we shall no longer be staggered at the greatness of the promise: "*Whatsoever* ye shall ask in My Name, I will do it." We shall get some insight into the unchangeable necessity and certainty of the law: what is asked in the Name of Christ, in union with Him, out of His nature and Spirit, must be given. As Christ's prayer-nature lives in us, His prayer-power becomes ours too. Not that the measure of our attainment or experience is the ground of our confidence, but the honesty and whole-heartedness of our surrender to all that we see that Christ seeks to be in us, will be the measure of our spiritual fitness and power to pray in His Name. "If ye abide in Me," He says, "ye shall ask what ye will." As we live in Him, we get the spiritual power to avail ourselves of His Name. As the branch wholly given up to the life and service of the Vine can count upon all its sap and strength for its fruit, so the believer, who in faith has accepted the fulness of the Spirit to possess his whole life, can indeed avail himself of all the power of Christ's Name.

Here on earth Christ as man came to reveal what prayer is. To pray in the Name of Christ we must pray as He prayed on earth; as He taught us to pray; in union with Him, as He now prays in heaven. We must in love study, and in faith accept, Him as our Example, our Teacher, our Intercessor.

### CHRIST OUR EXAMPLE.

Prayer in Christ on earth and in us cannot be two different things. Just as there is but one God, who is a Spirit, who hears prayer, there is but one spirit of acceptable prayer. When we realise what time Christ spent in prayer, and how the great events of His life were all connected with special prayer, we learn the necessity of absolute dependence on and unceasing direct communication with the heavenly world, if we are to live a heavenly life, or to exercise heavenly power around us. We see how foolish and fruitless the attempt must be to do work for God and heaven, without in the first place in prayer getting the life and the power of heaven to possess us. Unless this truth lives in us, we cannot avail ourselves aright of the mighty power of the Name of Christ. His example must teach us the meaning of His Name.

Of His baptism we read, "Jesus having been baptized, *and praying,* the heaven was opened." It was in prayer heaven was opened to Him, that heaven came down to Him with the Spirit and the voice of the Father. In the power of these He was led into the wilderness, in fasting and prayer to have them tested and fully appropriated. Early in His ministry Mark records (1:35), "And in the morning, a great while before day, He rose and departed into a desert place, *and there prayed.*" And somewhat later Luke tells (5:1), "Multitudes came together to hear and to be healed. *But He withdrew Himself into the desert, and prayed.*" He knew how the holiest service, preaching and healing, can exhaust the spirit; how too much intercourse with men could cloud the fellowship with God; how time, time, full time, is needed if the spirit is to rest and root in Him; how no pressure of duty among men can free from the absolute need of much prayer. If anyone could have been satisfied with always living and working in the spirit of prayer, it would have been our Master. But He could not; He needed to have His supplies replenished by continual and long-continued seasons of prayer. To use Christ's Name in prayer surely includes this, to follow His example and to pray as He did.

Of the night before choosing His apostles we read (Luke 6:12), "He went out into the mountain *to pray, and continued all night in prayer to God.*" The first step towards the constitution of the Church, and the separation of men to be His witnesses and successors, called Him to special long-continued prayer. All had to be done according to the pattern on the mount. "The Son can do nothing of Himself: the Father showeth Him all things that Himself doeth." It was in the night of prayer it was shown Him.

In the night between the feeding of the five thousand, when Jesus knew that they wanted to take Him by force and make Him King, and the walking on the sea, "He withdrew again into the mountain, Himself alone, *to pray*" (Matt. 1:23; Mark 6:46; John 6:15). It was God's will He was come to do, and God's power He was to show forth. He had it not as a possession of His own; it had to be prayed for and received from above. The first announcement of His approaching death, after He had elicited from Peter the confession that He was the Christ, is introduced by the words (Luke 9: 15), "And it came to pass that *He was praying alone.*" The introduction to the story of the Transfiguration is (Luke 9: 28), "He went up into the mountain *to pray.*" The request of the disciples, "Lord, teach us to pray" (Luke 11:1), follows on, "It came to pass *as He was praying* in a certain place." In His own personal life, in His intercourse with the Father, in all He is and does for men, the Christ whose name we are to use is a Man of prayer. It is prayer gives Him His power of blessing, and transfigures His very body with the glory of heaven. It is His own prayer-life makes Him the teacher of others how to pray. How much more must it be prayer, prayer alone, much prayer, that can fit us to share His glory of a transfigured life, or make us the channel of heavenly blessing and teaching to others. To pray in the Name of Christ is to pray as He prays.

As the end approaches, it is still more prayer. When the Greeks asked to see Him, and He spoke of His approaching death, He prayed. At Lazarus' grave He prayed. In the last night He prayed His prayer as our High-Priest, that we might know what His sacrifice would win, and what His everlasting intercession on the throne would be. In Gethsemane He prayed His prayer as Victim, the Lamb giving itself to the slaughter. On the Cross it is still all prayer—the prayer of compassion for His murderers; the prayer of atoning suffering in the thick darkness; the prayer in death of confiding resignation of His spirit to the Father. (Note E.)

Christ's life and work, His suffering and death—it was all prayer, all dependence on God, trust in God, receiving from God, surrender to God. Thy redemption, O believer, is a redemption wrought out by prayer and intercession: thy Christ is a praying Christ: the life He lives for thee, the life He lives in thee, is a praying life, that delights to wait on God and receive all from Him. To pray in His Name is to pray as He prayed. Christ is only our example because He is our Head, our Saviour, and our Life. In virtue of His Deity and of His Spirit He can live in us: we can pray in His Name, because we abide in Him and He in us.

## CHRIST OUR TEACHER.

Christ was what He taught. All His teaching was just the revelation of how He lived, and—praise God—of the life He was to live in us. His teaching of the disciples was first to awaken desire, and so prepare them for what He would by the Holy Spirit be and work in them. Let us believe very confidently: all He was in prayer, and all He taught, He Himself will give. He came to fulfil the law; much more will He fulfil the gospel in all He taught us, as to what to pray, and how.

*What to pray.*—It has sometimes been said that direct petitions, as compared with the exercise of fellowship with God, are but a subordinate part of prayer, and that "in the prayer of those who pray best and most, they occupy but an inconsiderable place." If we carefully study all that our Lord spoke of prayer, we shall see that this is not His teaching. In the Lord's Prayer, in the parables on prayer, in the illustration of a child asking bread, of our seeking and knocking, in the central thought of the prayer of faith, "Whatsoever ye pray, believe that ye have received," in the oft-repeated *"whatsoever"* of the last evening—everywhere our Lord urges and encourages us to offer definite petitions, and to expect definite answers. It is only because we have too much confined prayer to our own needs, that it has been thought needful to free it from the appearance of selfishness, by giving the petitions a subordinate place. If once believers were to awake to the glory of the work of intercession, and to see that in it, and the definite pleading for definite gifts on definite spheres and persons, lie our highest fellowship with our glorified Lord, and our only real power to bless men, it would be seen that there can be no truer fellowship with God than these definite petitions and their answers, by which we become the channel of His grace and life to men. Then our fellowship with the Father is even such as the Son has in His intercession.

*How to pray.*—Our Lord taught us to pray in secret, in simplicity, with the eye on God alone, in humility, in the spirit of forgiving love. But the chief truth He reiterated was ever this: to pray in faith. And He defined that faith, not only as a trust in God's goodness or power, but as the definite assurance that we have received the very thing we ask. And then, in view of the delay in the answer, He insisted on perseverance and urgency. We must be followers of those "who through faith and patience inherit the promises"—the faith that accepts the promise, and knows it has what it has asked —the patience that obtains the promise and inherits the blessing. We shall then learn to understand why God, who promises to avenge His elect speedily, bears with them in seeming delay. It is that their faith may be purified from all that is of the flesh, and tested and strengthened to become that spiritual power that can do all things—can even cast mountains into the heart of the sea.


### CHRIST AS OUR INTERCESSOR.

We have gazed on Christ in His prayers; we have listened to His teaching as to how we must pray; to know fully what it is to pray in His Name, we must know Him too in His heavenly intercession.

Just think what it means: that all His saving work wrought from heaven is still carried on, just as on earth, in unceasing communication with, and direct intercession to the Father, who worketh all in all, who is All in All. Every act of grace in Christ has been preceded by, and owes its power to, intercession. God has been honoured and acknowledged as its Author. On the throne of God, Christ's highest fellowship with the Father, and His partnership in His rule of the world, is in intercession. Every blessing that comes down to us from above bears upon it the stamp from God: through Christ's intercession. His intercession is nothing but the fruit and the glory of His atonement. When He gave Himself a sacrifice to God for men, He proved that His whole heart had the one object: the glory of God, in the salvation of men. In His intercession this great purpose is realised: He glorifies the Father by asking and receiving all of Him; He saves men by bestowing what He has obtained from the Father. Christ's intercession is the Father's glory, His own glory, our glory.

And now, this Christ, the Intercessor, is our life; He is our Head, and we are His body; His Spirit and life breathe in us. As in heaven so on earth, intercession is God's chosen, God's only channel of blessing. Let us learn from Christ what glory there is in it; what the way to exercise this wondrous power; what the part it is to take in work for God.

*The glory of it.*—By it, beyond anything, we glorify God. By it we glorify Christ. By it we bring blessing to the Church and the world. By it we obtain our highest nobility—the Godlike power of saving men.

*The way to it.*—Paul writes, "Walk in love, even as Christ loved us, and gave Himself a sacrifice to God for us." If we live as Christ lives, we will, as He did, give ourselves, for our whole life, to God, to be used by Him for men. When once we have done this, given ourselves, no more to seek anything for ourselves, but for men, and that to God, for Him to use us, and to impart to us what we can bestow on others, intercession will become to us, as it is in Christ in heaven, the great work of our life. And if ever the thought comes that the call is too high, or the work too great, the faith in Christ, the Interceding Christ, who lives in us, will give us the victory. We will listen to Him who said, "The works that I do, shall ye do; and greater works shall ye do." We shall remember that we are not under the law, with its impotence, but under grace with its omnipotence, working all in us. We shall believe again in Him who said to us, Rise and walk, and gave us— and we received it—His life as our strength. We shall claim afresh the fulness of God's Spirit as His sufficient provision for our need, and count Him to be in us the Spirit of Intercession, who makes us one with Christ in His. Oh! let us only keep our place—giving up ourselves, like Him, in Him, to God for men.

Then we shall understand the part intercession is to take in God's work through us. We shall no longer try to work for God, and ask Him to follow it with His blessing. We shall do what the friend at midnight did, what Christ did on earth, and ever does in heaven—we shall first get from God, and then turn to men to give what He gave us. As with Christ, we shall make our chief work, we shall count no time or trouble too great, to receive from the Father; giving to men will then be in power.

Servants of Christ! children of God! be of good courage. Let no fear of feebleness or poverty make you afraid—ask in the Name of Christ. His Name is Himself, in all His perfection and power. He is the living Christ, and will Himself make His Name a power in you. Fear not to plead the Name: His promise is a threefold cord that cannot be broken: *Whatsoever ye ask—in My Name*—IT SHALL BE DONE UNTO YOU.

# *12*

## MY GOD WILL HEAR ME

"Therefore will the Lord wait, that He may be gracious unto you. Blessed are all they that wait for Him. He will be very gracious unto thee at the voice of thy cry; when He shall hear it, He will answer thee."—Isa. 30:18, 19.

"The Lord will hear when *I call* upon Him."—Ps. 4:3.

"I have called upon Thee, for Thou *wilt hear me,* O God!"—Ps. 17:6.

"I will look unto the Lord; I will wait for the God of my salvation: my God *will hear me.*"—Mic. 7:7.

THE power of prayer rests in the faith that God hears it. In more than one sense this is true. It is this faith that gives a man courage to pray. It is this faith that gives him power to prevail with God. The moment I am assured that God hears *me* too, I feel drawn to pray and to persevere in prayer. I feel strong to claim and to take in faith the answer God gives. One great reason of lack of prayer is the want of the living, joyous assurance: "My God will hear me." If once God's servants got a vision of the living God waiting to grant their request, and to bestow all the heavenly gifts of the Spirit they are in need of, for themselves or those they are serving, how everything would be set aside to make time and room for this one only power that can ensure heavenly blessing—the prayer of faith!

When a man can, and does say, in living faith, "My God will hear me!" surely nothing can keep him from prayer. He knows that what he cannot do or get done on earth, can and will be done for him from heaven. Let each one of us bow in stillness before God, and wait on Him to reveal Himself as the prayer-bearing God. In His presence the wondrous thoughts gathering round the central truth will unfold themselves to us.

1. *"My God will hear me."—What a blessed certainty!—* We have God's word for it in numberless promises. We have thousands of witnesses to the fact that they have found it true. We have had experience of it in our lives. We have had the Son of God come from heaven with the message that if we ask, the Father will give. We have had Himself praying on earth, and being heard. And we have Him in heaven now, sitting at the right hand of God and making intercession for us. God hears prayer—God delights to hear prayer. He has allowed His people a thousand times over to be tried, that they might be compelled to cry to Him, and learn to know Him as the Hearer of Prayer.

Let us confess with shame how little we have believed this wondrous truth, in the sense of receiving it into our heart, and allowing it to possess and control our whole being. That we accept a truth is not enough; the living God, of whom the truth speaks, must in its light so be revealed, that our whole life is spent in His presence, with the consciousness as clear as in a little child towards its earthly parent—I know for certain my father hears me.

Beloved child of God! you know by experience how little an intellectual apprehension of truth has profited you. Beseech God to reveal Himself to you. If you want to live a different prayer-life, bow each time ere you pray in silence to worship this God; to wait till there rests on you some right sense of His nearness and readiness to answer. So will you begin to pray with the words, "My God will hear me!"

2. *"My God will hear me." What a wondrous grace!—* Think of God in His infinite majesty, His altogether incomprehensible glory, His unapproachable holiness, sitting on a throne of grace, waiting to be gracious, inviting, encouraging you to pray with His promise: "Call upon Me, and I will answer thee." Think of yourself, in your nothingness and helplessness as a creature; in your wretchedness and transgressions as a sinner; in your feebleness and unworthiness as a saint; and praise the glory of that grace which allows you to say boldly of your prayer for yourself and others, "My

God will hear me." Think of how you are not left to yourself, and what you can accomplish, in this wonderful intercourse with God. God has united you with Christ; in Him and His Name you have your confidence; on the throne He prays with you and for you; on the footstool of the throne you pray with Him and in Him. His worth, and the Father's delight in hearing Him, are the measure of your confidence, your assurance of being heard. There is more. Think of the Holy Spirit, the Spirit of God's own Son, sent into your heart to cry, Abba, Father, and to be *in you* a Spirit of Supplication, when you know not what to pray as you ought. Think, in all your insignificance and unworthiness, of your being as acceptable as Christ Himself. Think in all your ignorance and feebleness, of the Spirit making intercession according to God within you, and cry out, "What wondrous grace! Through Christ I have access to the Father, by the Spirit. I can, I do believe it: 'My God will hear me.' "

3. *"My God will hear me."—What a deep mystery!—* There are difficulties that cannot but at times arise and perplex even the honest heart. There is the question as to God's sovereign, all-wise, all-disposing will. How can our wishes, often so foolish, and our will, often so selfish, overrule or change that perfect will? Were it not better to leave all to His disposal, who knows what is best, and loves to give us the very best? Or how can our prayer change what He has ordained before? Then there is the question as to the need of persevering prayer, and long waiting for the answer. If God be Infinite Love, and delighting more to give than we to receive, where the need for the pleading and wrestling, the urgency, and the long delay of which Scripture and experience speak? Arising out of this there is still another question —that of the multitude of apparently vain and unanswered prayers. How many have pleaded for loved ones, and they die unsaved. How many cry for years for spiritual blessing, and no answer comes. To think of all this tries our faith, and makes us hesitate as we say, "My God will hear me."

Beloved! prayer, in its power with God, and His faithfulness to His promise to hear it, is a deep spiritual mystery. To the questions put above answers can be given that remove some of the difficulty. But, after all, the first and the last that must be said is this: As little as we can comprehend God can we comprehend this, one of the most blessed of His attributes, that He hears prayer. It is a spiritual mystery— nothing less than the mystery of the Holy Trinity. God hears because we pray in His Son, because the Holy Spirit prays in us. If we have believed and claimed the life of Christ as our health, and the fulness of the Spirit as our strength, let us not hesitate to believe in the power of our prayer too. The Holy Spirit can enable us to believe and rejoice in it, even where every question is not yet answered. He will do this, as we lay our questionings in God's bosom, trust His faithfulness, and give ourselves humbly to obey His command to pray without ceasing. Every art unfolds its secrets and its beauty only to the man who practises it. To the humble soul who prays in the obedience of faith, who practises prayer and intercession diligently, because God asks it, the secret of the Lord will be revealed, and the thought of the deep mystery of prayer, instead of being a weary problem, will be a source of rejoic- ing, adoration, and faith, in which the unceasing refrain is ever heard: *"My God will hear me!"*

4. *"My God will hear me." What a solemn responsibility!* —How often we complain of darkness, of feebleness, of failure, as if there was no help for it. And God has promised in answer to our prayer to supply our every need, and give us His light and strength and peace. Would that we realised the responsibility of having such a God, and such promises, with the sin and shame of not availing ourselves of them to the utmost. How confident we should feel that the grace, which we have accepted and trusted to enable us to pray as we should, will be given.

There is more. This access to a prayer-hearing God is specially meant to make us intercessors for our fellow-men. Even as Christ obtained His right of prevailing intercession by His giving Himself a sacrifice to God for men, and through it receives the blessings He dispenses, so, if we have truly with Christ given ourselves to God for men, we share His right of intercession, and are able to obtain the powers of the heavenly world for them too. The power of life and death is in our hand (1 John 5:16). In answer to prayer the Spirit can be poured out, souls can be converted, believers can be established. In prayer the kingdom of darkness can be conquered, souls brought out of prison into the liberty of Christ, and the glory of God be revealed. Through prayer, the sword of the Spirit, which is the Word of God, can be wielded in power, and, in public preaching as in private speaking, the most rebellious made to bow at Jesus' feet.

What a responsibility on the Church to give herself to the work of intercession! What a responsibility on every minister, missionary, worker, set apart for the saving of souls, to yield himself wholly to act out and prove his faith: "My God will hear me!" And what a call on every believer, instead of burying and losing this talent, to seek to the very utmost to use it in prayer and supplication for all saints and for all men. My God will hear me: The deeper our entrance into the truth of this wondrous power God hath given to men, the more whole-hearted will be our surrender to the work of intercession.

5. *"My God will hear me." What a blessed prospect!*—I see it—all the failures of my past life have been owing to the lack of this faith. My failure, especially in the work of intercession, has had its deepest root in this—I did not live in the full faith of the blessed assurance, *"My God will hear me!"* Praise God! I begin to see it—I believe it. All can be different. Or, rather, I see Him, I believe Him. *"My God will hear me!"* Yes, me, even me! Commonplace and insignificant though I be, filling but a very little place, so that I will scarce be missed when I go—even I have access to this Infinite God, with the confidence that He heareth me. One with Christ, led by the Holy Spirit, I dare to say: "I will pray for others, for I am sure my God will listen to me: *'My God will hear me!'*" What a blessed prospect before me—every earthly and spiritual anxiety exchanged for the peace of God, who cares for all and hears prayer. What a blessed prospect in my work —to know that even when the answer is long delayed, and there is a call for much patient, persevering prayer, the truth remains infallibly sure—*"My God will hear me!"*

And what a blessed prospect for Christ's Church if we

could but all give prayer its place, give faith in God its place, or, rather, *give the prayer-hearing God His place!* Is not this the one great thing, those, who in some little measure begin to see the urgent need of prayer, ought in the first place to pray for. When God, at the first, time after time, poured forth the Spirit on His praying people, He laid down the law for all time: as much of prayer, so much of the Spirit. Let each one who can say, "*My God will hear me*," join in the fervent supplication, that throughout the Church that truth may be restored to its true place, and the blessed prospect will be realised: a praying Church endued with the power of the Holy Ghost.

6. "*My God will hear me.*" *What a need of Divine teaching!*—We need this, both to enable us to hold this word in living faith, and to make full use of it in intercession. It has been said, and it cannot be said too often or too earnestly, that the one thing needful for the Church of our day is, the power of the Holy Spirit. It is just because this is so, from the Divine side, that we may also say as truly that, from the human side, the one thing needful is, more prayer, more believing, persevering prayer. In speaking of lack of the Spirit's power, and the condition for receiving it, someone used the expression—the block is not on the perpendicular, but on the horizontal line. It is to be feared that it is on both. There is much to be confessed and taken away in us if the Spirit is to work freely. But it is specially on the perpendicular line that the block is—the upward look, and the deep dependence, and the strong crying to God, and the effectual prayer of faith that avails—all this is sadly lacking. And just this is the one thing useful.

Shall we not all set ourselves to learn the lesson which will make prevailing prayer possible—the lesson of a faith that always sings, "*My God will hear me*"? Simple and elementary as it is, it needs practice and patience, it needs time and heavenly teaching, to learn it aright. Under the impression of a bright thought, or a blessed experience, it may look as if we knew the lesson perfectly. But ever again the need will recur of making this our first prayer—that God who hears prayer would teach us to believe it, and so to pray aright.

If we desire it we can count upon Him, He who delights in hearing prayer and answering it, He who gave His Son that He might ever pray for us and with us, and His Holy Spirit to pray in us, we can be sure there is not a prayer that He will hear more certainly than this: that He so reveal Himself as the prayer-hearing God, that our whole being may respond, *"My God will hear me."*

# 13

## PAUL A PATTERN OF PRAYER

"Go and inquire for one called Saul of Tarsus: for, *behold, he prayeth.*"—Acts 9:11.

"For this cause I obtained mercy, that in me first Jesus Christ might show forth all long-suffering, for a pattern to them which should hereafter believe on Him to life everlasting."—1 Tim. 1:16.

God took His own Son, and made Him our Example and our Pattern. It sometimes is as if the power of Christ's example is lost in the thought that He, in whom is no sin, is not man as we are. Our Lord took Paul, a man of like passions with ourselves, and made him a pattern of what he could do for one who was the chief of sinners. And Paul, the man who, more than any other, has set his mark on the Church, has ever been appealed to as a pattern man. In his mastery of Divine truth, and his teaching of it; in his devotion to his Lord, and his self-consuming zeal in His service; in his deep experience of the power of the indwelling Christ and the fellowship of His cross; in the sincerity of his humility, and the simplicity and boldness of his faith; in his missionary enthusiasm and endurance—in all this, and so much more, "the grace of our Lord Jesus was exceeding abundant in him." Christ gave him, and the Church has accepted him, as a pattern of what Christ would have, of what Christ would work. Seven times Paul speaks of believers following him: (1 Cor. 4:16), "Wherefore I beseech you, be ye followers of me"; (11:1), "Be ye followers of me, even as I am of Christ"; Phil. 3:17, 4:9; 1 Thess. 1:6; 2 Thess. 3:7-9.

If Paul, as a pattern of prayer, is not as much studied or appealed to as he is in other respects, it is not because he is not in this too as remarkable a proof of what grace can do, or because we do not, in this respect, as much stand in need of the help of his example. A study of Paul as a pattern of prayer will bring a rich reward of instruction and encouragement. The words our Lord used of him at his conversion, "Behold he prayeth," may be taken as the keynote of his life. The heavenly vision which brought him to his knees ever after ruled his life. Christ at the right hand of God, in whom we are blessed with all spiritual blessings, was everything to him; to pray and expect the heavenly power in his work and on his work, from heaven direct by prayer, was the simple outcome of his faith in the Glorified One. In this, too, Christ meant him to be a pattern, that we might learn that, just in the measure in which the heavenliness of Christ and His gifts, the unworldliness of the powers that work for salvation, are known and believed, will prayer become the spontaneous rising of the heart to the only source of its life. Let us see what we know of Paul.

## PAUL'S HABITS OF PRAYER.

These are revealed almost unconsciously. He writes (Rom. 1:9), "God is my witness, that without ceasing I make mention of you *always in my prayers.* For I long to see you, that I may impart unto you some spiritual gift, to the end ye may be established." Rom. 10:1, 4:2, 3: "My *heart's desire and prayer to God* for Israel is, that they may be saved"; "I have great heaviness and *continual sorrow of heart*; for I could wish that myself were accursed from Christ for my brethren." 1 Cor. 1:4: "I thank my God *always* on your behalf, for the grace of God which is given you by Jesus Christ." 2 Cor. 6: 4, 6: "Approving ourselves as the ministers of Christ, *in watchings, in fastings.*" Gal. 4:19: "My little children, of whom *I travail in birth again* till Christ be formed in you." Eph. 1:16: "*I cease not* to give thanks for you, making mention of you *in my prayers.*" Eph. 3:14: "*I bow my knees* to the Father, that He would grant you to be strengthened with might by His Spirit in the inner man." Phil. 1: 3, 4, 8, 9: "I thank my God *upon every remembrance of you, always in every prayer of mine* making request for you all with joy. For God is my record, how greatly I long after you all in the bowels of Jesus Christ. And this *I pray*"—Col. 1:3, 9: "We give thanks to God, *praying always for you.* For this cause also, since the day we heard it, we *do not cease to pray for you,* and to desire"—Col. 2:1: "I would that ye knew what *great conflict* I have for you, and for as many as have not seen my face in the flesh." 1 Thess. 1:2: "We give thanks to God *always* for you all, making mention of you *in our prayers.*" 3:9: "We joy for your sakes before God; *night and day praying exceedingly* that we might perfect that which is lacking in your faith." 2 Thess. 1:3: "We are bound to thank God *always* for you. Wherefore also *we always pray* for you." 2 Tim. 1:3: "I thank God, that *without easing* I have remembrance of thee night and day." Philem. 4: "I thank my God, making mention of thee *always in my prayers.*"

These passages taken together give us the picture of a man whose words, "Pray without ceasing," were simply the expression of his daily life. He had such a sense of the insufficiency of simple conversion; of the need of the grace and the power of heaven being brought down for the young converts in prayer; of the need of much and unceasing prayer, day and night, to bring it down; of the certainty that prayer would bring it down—that his life was continual and most definite prayer. He had such a sense that everything must come from above, and such a faith that it would come in answer to prayer, that prayer was neither a duty nor a burden, but the natural turning of the heart to the only place whence it could possibly obtain what it sought for others.

### THE CONTENTS OF PAUL'S PRAYERS.

It is of as much importance to know *what* Paul prayed, as how frequently and earnestly he did so. Intercession is a spiritual work. Our confidence in it will depend much on our knowing that we ask according to the will of God. The more distinctly we ask heavenly things, which we feel at once God alone can bestow, which we are sure He will bestow, the more direct and urgent will our appeal be to God alone. The more impossible the things are that we seek, the more we will turn from all human work to prayer and to God alone.

In the Epistles, in addition to expressions in which he speaks of his praying, we have a number of distinct prayers in which Paul gives utterance to his heart's desire for those to whom he writes. In these we see that his first desire was always that they might be "established" in the Christian life. Much as he praised God when he heard of conversion, he knew how feeble the young converts were, and how for their establishing nothing would avail without the grace of the Spirit prayed down. If we notice some of the principal of these prayers we shall see what he asked and obtained.

Take the two prayers in Ephesians—the one for light, the other for strength. In the former (1 : 15), he prays for the Spirit of wisdom to enlighten them to know what their calling was, what their inheritance, what the mighty power of God working in them. Spiritual enlightenment and knowledge was their great need, to be obtained for them by prayer. In the latter (3 : 15) he asks that the power they had been led to see in Christ might work in them, and they be strengthened with Divine might, so as to have the indwelling Christ, and the love that passeth knowledge, and the fulness of God actually come on them. These were things that could only come direct from heaven; these were things he asked and expected. If we want to learn Paul's art of intercession, we must ask nothing less for believers in our days.

Look at the prayer in Philippians (1 : 9-11). There, too, it is first for spiritual knowledge; then comes a blameless life, and then a fruitful life to the glory of God. So also in the beautiful prayer in Colossians (1 : 9-11). First, spiritual knowledge and understanding of God's will, then the strengthening with all might to all patience and joy.

Or take the two prayers in 1 Thessalonians (3 : 12, 13, and 5 : 23). The one: "God so increase your love to one another, that He may stablish your *hearts unblameable in holiness.*" The other: "God *sanctify you wholly,* and preserve you blameless." The very words are so high that we hardly understand, still less believe, still less experience what they mean. Paul so lived in the heavenly world, he was so at home in the holiness and omnipotence of God and His love, that such prayers were the natural expression of what he knew God could and would do. "God stablish your hearts unblameable in holiness," "God sanctify you wholly"—the man who believes in these things and desires them, will pray for them for others. The prayers are all a proof that he seeks for them the very life of heaven upon earth. No wonder that he is not tempted to trust in any human means, but looks for it from heaven alone. Again, I say, the more we take Paul's prayers as our pattern, and make his desires our own for believers for whom we pray, the more will prayer to the God of heaven become as our daily breath.

### PAUL'S REQUESTS FOR PRAYER.

These are no less instructive than his own prayers for the saints. They prove that he does not count prayer any special prerogative of an apostle; he calls the humblest and simplest believer to claim his right. They prove that he does not think that only the new converts or feeble Christians need prayer; he himself is, as a member of the body, dependent upon his brethren and their prayers. After he had preached the gospel for twenty years, he still asks for prayer that he may speak as he ought to speak. Not once for all, not for a time, but day by day, and that without ceasing, must grace be sought and brought down from heaven for his work. United, continued waiting on God is to Paul the only hope of the Church. With the Holy Spirit a heavenly life, the life of the Lord in heaven, entered the world; nothing but unbroken communication with heaven can keep it up.

Listen how he asks for prayer, and with what earnestness—Rom. 15:30: "*I beseech you*, brethren, for the Lord Jesus Christ's sake, and for the love of the Spirit, that ye *strive together with me in your prayers* to God for me; that I may be delivered from them which do not believe in Judea; and may come unto you with joy by the will of God." How remarkably both prayers were answered: Rom. 15:5, 6, 13. The remarkable fact that the Roman world-power, which in Pilate with Christ, in Herod with Peter, at Philippi, had proved its antagonism to God's kingdom, all at once becomes Paul's protector, and secures him a safe convoy to Rome, can only be accounted for by these prayers.

2 Cor. 1:10, 11: "In whom we trust that He will yet deliver us, *ye also helping together by prayer* for us." Eph. 6:18, 19: "Praying always with all prayer and supplication in the Spirit, for all saints; *and for me* that I may open my mouth boldly, that therein I may speak boldly as I ought to speak." Phil. 1:19: "I know that this (trouble) shall turn to my salvation, *through your prayer,* and the supply of the Spirit of Jesus Christ." Col. 4:2, 3, 4: "Continue in prayer; withal also *praying for us,* that God would open unto us a door of utterance, to speak the mystery of Christ: that I may make it manifest as I ought to speak." 1 Thess. 5:25: "Brethren, pray for us." Philem. 22: "I trust that through your prayers I shall be given to you."

We saw how Christ prayed, and taught His disciples to pray. We see how Paul prayed, and taught the churches to pray. As the Master, so the servant calls us to believe and to prove that prayer is the power alike of the ministry and the Church. Of his faith we have a summary in these remarkable words concerning something that caused him grief: "This shall turn to my salvation through your prayer, and the supply of the Spirit of Jesus Christ." As much as he looked to his Lord in heaven did he look to his brethren on earth, to secure the supply of that Spirit for him. The Spirit from heaven and prayer on earth were to him, as to the twelve after Pentecost, inseparably linked. We speak often of apostolic zeal and devotion and power—may God give us a revival of apostolic prayer.

Let me once again ask the question: Does the work of intercession take the place in the Church it ought to have? Is it a thing commonly understood in the Lord's work, that everything depends upon getting from God that "supply of the Spirit of Christ" for and in ourselves that can give our work its real power to bless. This is Christ's Divine order for all work, His own and that of His servants; this is the order Paul followed: first come every day, as having nothing, and receive from God "the supply of the Spirit" in intercession—then go and impart what has come to thee from heaven.

In all His instructions, our Lord Jesus spake much oftener to His disciples about their praying than their preaching. In the farewell discourse, He said little about preaching, but much about the Holy Spirit, and their asking whatsoever they would in His Name. If we are to return to this life of the first apostles and of Paul, and really accept the truth every day—my first work, my only strength is intercession, to secure the power of God on the souls entrusted to me—we must have the courage to confess past sin, and to believe that there is deliverance. To break through old habits, to resist the clamour of pressing duties that have always had their way, to make every other call subordinate to this one, whether others approve or not, will not be easy at first. But the men or women who are faithful will not only have a reward themselves, but become benefactors to their brethren. "Thou shalt be called the repairer of the breach, the restorer of paths to dwell in."

But is it really possible? Can it indeed be that those who have never been able to face, much less to overcome the difficulty, can yet become mighty in prayer? Tell me, was it really possible for Jacob to become Israel—a prince who prevailed with God? It was. The things that are impossible with men are possible with God. Have you not in very deed received from the Father, as the great fruit of Christ's redemption, the Spirit of supplication, the Spirit of intercession? Just pause and think what that means. And will you still doubt whether God is able to make you "strivers with God," princes who prevail with Him? Oh, let us banish all fear, and in faith claim the grace for which we have the Holy Spirit dwelling in us, the grace of supplication, the grace of intercession. Let us quietly, perseveringly believe that He lives in us, and will enable us to do our work. Let us in faith not fear to accept and yield to the great truth that intercession, as it is the great work of the King on the throne, *is the great work of His servants on earth.* We have the Holy Spirit, who brings the Christ-life into our hearts, to fit us for this work. Let us at once begin and stir up the gift within us. As we set aside each day our time for intercession, and count upon the Spirit's enabling power, the confidence will grow that we can, in our measure, follow Paul even as he followed Christ.

# *14*

## GOD SEEKS INTERCESSORS

"I have set watchmen upon thy walls, O Jerusalem, which shall never hold their peace day nor night. Ye that are the Lord's remembrancers, keep not silence, and give Him no rest till He make Jerusalem a praise in the earth." —ISA. 62:6, 7.

"And He saw that there was *no man,* and wondered that there was *no intercessor.*"—ISA. 59:16.

"And I looked, and there was *none to help*; and I wondered, and there was *none to uphold.*"—ISA. 63:5.

"There is *none* that calleth upon Thy name, that stirreth himself to take hold of Thee."—ISA. 64:7.

"And I sought for a man that should stand in the gap before Me for the land, that I should not destroy it; but *I found none.*"—EZEK. 22:30.

"I chose you, and appointed you, that ye should go and bear fruit: that whatsoever ye shall ask of the Father in My name, He may give it you."—JOHN 15:16.

IN the study of the starry heavens, how much depends upon a due apprehension of magnitudes. Without some sense of the size of the heavenly bodies, that appear so small to the eye, and yet are so great, and of the almost illimitable extent of the regions in which they move, though they appear so near and so familiar, there can be no true knowledge of the heavenly world or its relation to this earth. It is even so with the spiritual heavens, and the heavenly life in which we are called to live. It is specially so in the life of intercession, that most wondrous intercourse between heaven and earth. Everything depends upon the due apprehension of magnitudes.

Just think of the three that come first: There is a world,

111

with its needs entirely dependent on and waiting to be helped by intercession; there is a God in heaven, with His all-sufficient supply for all those needs, waiting to be asked; there is a Church, with its wondrous calling and its sure promises, waiting to be roused to a sense of its wondrous responsibility and power.

*God seeks intercessors.*—There is a world with its perishing millions, with intercession as its only hope. How much of love and work is comparatively vain, because there is so little intercession. A thousand millions living as if there never had been a Son of God to die for them. Thirty millions every year passing into the outer darkness without hope. Fifty millions bearing the Christian name, and the great majority living in utter ignorance or indifference. Millions of feeble, sickly Christians; thousands of wearied workers, who could be blessed by intercession, could help themselves to become mighty in intercession. Churches and missions sacrificing life and labour often with little result, for lack of intercession. Souls, each one worth more than worlds, worth nothing less than the price paid for them in Christ's blood, and within reach of the power that can be won by intercession. We surely have no conception of the magnitude of the work to be done by God's intercessors, or we should cry to God above everything to give from heaven the spirit of intercession.

*God seeks intercessors.*—There is a God of glory able to meet all these needs. We are told that He delights in mercy, that He waits to be gracious, that He longs to pour out His blessing; that the love that gave the Son to death is the measure of the love that each moment hovers over every human being. And yet He does not help. And there they perish, a million a month in China alone, and it is as if God does not move. If He does so love and long to bless, there must be some inscrutable reason for His holding back. What can it be? Scripture says, because of your unbelief. It is the faithlessness and consequent unfaithfulness of God's people. He has taken them up into partnership with Himself; He has honoured them, and bound Himself, by making their prayers one of the standard measures of the working of His power. Lack of intercession is one of the chief causes of lack of blessing. Oh, that we would turn eye and heart from everything else and fix them upon this God who hears prayer, until the magnificence of His promises, and His power, and His purpose of love overwhelmed us! How our whole life and heart would become intercession.

*God seeks intercessors.*—There is a third magnitude to which our eyes must be opened: the wondrous privilege and power of the intercessors. There is a false humility, which makes a great virtue of self-depreciation, because it has never seen its utter nothingness. If it knew that, it would never apologise for its feebleness, but glory in its utter weakness, as the one condition of Christ's power resting on it. It would judge of itself, its power and influence before God in prayer, as little by what it sees or feels, as we judge of the size of the sun or stars by what the eye can see. Faith sees man created in God's image and likeness to be God's representative in this world and have dominion over it. Faith sees man redeemed and lifted into union with Christ, abiding in Him, identified with Him, and clothed with His power in intercession. Faith sees the Holy Spirit dwelling and praying in the heart, making, in our sighings, intercession according to God. Faith sees the intercession of the saints to be part of the life of the Holy Trinity—the believer as God's child asking of the Father, in the Son, through the Spirit. Faith sees something of the Divine fitness and beauty of this scheme of salvation through intercession, wakens the soul to a consciousness of its wondrous destiny, and girds it with strength for the blessed self-sacrifice it calls to.

*God seeks intercessors.*—When He called His people out of Egypt, He separated the priestly tribe, to draw nigh to Him, and stand before Him, and bless the people in His name. From time to time He sought and found and honoured intercessors, for whose sake He spared or blessed His people. When our Lord left the earth He said to the inner circle He had gathered around Him—an inner circle of special devotion to His service, to which access is still free to every disciple: "I chose you, and appointed you, that whatsoever ye shall ask of the Father in My Name, He may give it you." We have already noticed the six times repeated three wonderful words—*What-*

113

*soever—In My Name—It shall be done*. In them Christ placed the powers of the heavenly world at their disposal—not for their own selfish use, but in the interests of His kingdom. How wondrously they used it we know. And since that time, down through the ages, these men have had their successors, men who have proved how surely God works in answer to prayer. And we may praise God that in our days too, there is an ever-increasing number who begin to see and prove that in church and mission, in large societies and little circles and individual effort, intercession is the chief thing, the power that moves God and opens heaven. They are learning, and long to learn better, and that all may learn, that in all work for souls intercession must take the first place, and that those who in it have received from heaven, in the power of the Holy Ghost, what they are to communicate to others, will be best able to do the Lord's work.

*God seeks intercessors.*—Though God had His appointed servants in Israel, watchmen set by Himself to cry to Him day and night and give Him no rest, He often had to wonder and complain that there was no intercessor, none to stir himself up to take hold of His strength. And He still waits and wonders in our day, that there are not more intercessors, that all His children do not give themselves to this highest and holiest work, that many of them who do so, do not engage in it more intensely and perseveringly. He wonders to find ministers of His gospel complaining that their duties do not allow them to find time for this, which He counts their first, their highest, their most delightful, their alone effective work. He wonders to find His sons and daughters, who have forsaken home and friends for His sake and the gospel's, come so short in what He meant to be their abiding strength —receiving day by day all they needed to impart to the dark heathen. He wonders to find multitudes of His children who have hardly any conception of what intercession is. He wonders to find multitudes more who have learned that it is their duty, and seek to obey it, but confess that they know but little of taking hold upon God or prevailing with Him.

*God seeks intercessors.*—He longs to dispense larger blessings. He longs to reveal His power and glory as God,

His saving love, more abundantly. He seeks intercessors in larger number, in greater power, to prepare the way of the Lord. He seeks them. Where could He seek them but in His Church? And how does He expect to find them? He intrusted to His Church the task of telling of their Lord's need, the task of encouraging and training, and preparing them for His holy service. And He ever comes again, seeking fruit, seeking intercessors. In His Word He has spoken of the "widows indeed, who trust in God, and continue in supplication night and day." He looks if the Church is training the great army of aged men and women, whose time of outward work is past, but who can strenghen the army of the "elect, who cry to Him day and night." He looks to the great host of the Christian Endeavour, the three or four million of young lives that have given themselves away in the solemn pledge, "I promise the Lord Jesus Christ that I will strive to do whatever He would like to have me do," and wonders how many are being trained to pass from the brightness of the weekly prayer-meeting and its confession of loyalty, to swell the secret intercession that is to save souls. He looks to the thousands of young men and young women in training for the work of ministry and mission, and gazes longingly to see if the Church is teaching them that intercession, power with God, must be their first care, and in seeking to train and help them to it. He looks to see whether ministers and missionaries are understanding their opportunity, and labouring to train the believers of their congregation into those who can "help together" by their prayer, and can "strive with them in their prayers." As Christ seeks the lost sheep until He find it, Gods seeks intercessors. (Note F.)

*God seeks intercessors.*—He will not, He cannot, take the work out of the hands of His Church. And so He comes, calling and pleading in many ways. Now by a man whom He raises up to live a life of faith in His service, and to prove how actually and abundantly He answers prayer. Then by the story of a church which makes prayer for souls its starting-point, and bears testimony to God's faithfulness. Sometimes in a mission which proves how special prayer can meet special need, and bring down the power of the Spirit. And sometimes again by a season of revival coming in answer to united urgent supplication. In these and many other ways God is showing us what intercession can do, and beseeching us to waken up and train His great host to be, every one, a people of intercessors.

*God seeks intercessors.*—He sends His servants out to call them. Let ministers make this a part of their duty. Let them make their church a training school of intercession. Give the people definite objects for prayer. Encourage them to take a definite time to it, if it were only ten minutes every day. Help them to understand the boldness they may use with God. Teach them to expect and look out for answers. Show them what it is first to pray and get an answer in secret, and then carry the answer and impart the blessing. Tell everyone who is master of his own time that he is as the angels, free to tarry before the throne and then go out and minister to the heirs of salvation. Sound out the blessed tidings that this honour is for all God's people. There is no difference. That servant girl, this day labourer, that bedridden invalid, this daughter in her mother's home, these men and young men in business—all are called, all, all are needed. God seeks intercessors.

*God seeks intercessors.*—As ministers take up the work of finding and training them it will urge themselves to pray more. Christ gave Paul to be a pattern of His grace before He made him a preacher of it. It has been well said, "The first duty of a clergyman is humbly to beg of God that all he would have done in his people may be first truly and fully done in himself." The effort to bring this message of God may cause much heart-searching and humiliation. All the better. The best practice in doing a thing is helping others to do it. O ye servants of Christ, set as watchmen to cry to God day and night, let us awake to our holy calling. Let us believe in the power of intercession. Let us practise it. Let us seek on behalf of our people to get from God Himself the Spirit and the Life we preach. With our spirit and life given up to God in intercession, the Spirit and Life that God gives them through us cannot fail to be the Life of Intercession too.

# 15

## THE COMING REVIVAL

"Wilt Thou not revive us again: that Thy people may rejoice in Thee?"—Ps. 85:6.

"O Lord, revive Thy work in the midst of the years."—Hab. 3:2.

"Though I walk in the midst of trouble, Thou wilt revive me: Thy right hand shall save me."—Ps. 138:7.

"I dwell with him that is of a humble and contrite heart, to revive the heart of the contrite ones."—Isa. 57:15.

"Come, and let us return to the Lord: for He hath torn, and He will heal us. He will revive us."—Hos. 6:1, 2.

THE COMING REVIVAL—one frequently hears the word. There are teachers not a few who see the tokens of its approach, and confidently herald its speedy appearance. In the increase of mission interest, in the tidings of revivals in places where all were dead or cold, in the hosts of our young gathered into Students' and other Associations or Christian Endeavour Societies, in doors everywhere opened in the Christian and the heathen world, in victories already secured in the fields white unto the harvest, wherever believing, hopeful workers enter, they find the assurance of a time of power and blessing such as we have not known. The Church is about to enter on a new era of increasing spirituality and larger extension.

There are others who, while admitting the truth of some of these facts, yet fear that the conclusions drawn from them are one-sided and premature. They see the interest in missions increased, but point out to how small a circle it is confined, and how utterly out of proportion it is to what it ought to be. To the great majority of Church members, to the greater part of the Church, it is as yet anything but a life question. They remind us of the power of worldliness and formality, of the increase of the money-making and pleasure-loving spirit among professing Christians, to the lack of spirituality in so many, many of our churches, and the continuing and apparently increasing estrangement of multitudes from God's Day and Word, as proof that the great revival has certainly not begun, and is hardly thought of by the most. They say that they do not see the deep humiliation, the intense desire, the fervent prayer which appear as the forerunners of every true revival.

There are right-hand and left-hand errors which are equally dangerous. We must seek as much to be kept from the superficial Optimism, which never is able to gauge the extent of the evil, as from the hopeless Pessimism which can neither praise God for what He has done, nor trust Him for what He is ready to do. The former will lose itself in a happy self-gratulation, as it rejoices in its zeal and diligence and apparent success, and never see the need of confession and great striving in prayer, ere we are prepared to meet and conquer the hosts of darkness. The latter virtually gives over the world to Satan, and almost prays and rejoices to see things get worse, to hasten the coming of Him who is to put all right. May God keep us from either error, and fulfil the promise, "Thine ears shall hear a word behind thee, saying, This is the way, walk ye in it, when ye turn to the right hand, and when ye turn to the left." Let us listen to the lessons suggested by the passages we have quoted; they may help us to pray the prayer aright: "Revive Thy work, O Lord!"

1. *"Revive Thy work, O Lord!"*—Read again the passages of Scripture, and see how they all contain the one thought: Revival is God's work; He alone can give it; it must come from above. We are frequently in danger of looking to what God has done and is doing, and to count on that as the pledge that He will at once do more. And all the time it may be true that He is blessing us up to the measure of our faith or self-sacrifice, and cannot give larger measure, until there has been a new discovery and confession of what is hindering Him. Or

we may be looking to all the signs of life and good around us, and congratulating ourselves on all the organisations and agencies that are being created, while the need of God's mighty and direct interposition is not rightly felt, and the entire dependence upon Him not cultivated. Regeneration, the giving of Divine life, we all acknowledge to be God's act, a miracle of His power. The restoring or reviving of the Divine life, in a soul or a Church, is as much a supernatural work. To have the spiritual discernment that can understand the signs of the heavens, and prognosticate the coming revival, we need to enter deep into God's mind and will as to its conditions, and the preparedness of those who pray for it or are to be used to bring it about. 'Surely the Lord God will do nothing, but He revealeth His secret unto His servants the prophets.'' It is God who is to give the revival; it is God who reveals His secret; it is the spirit of absolute dependence upon God, giving Him the honour and the glory, that will prepare for it.

2. *"Revive Thy work, O Lord!"*—A second lesson suggested is, that the revival God is to give will be given in answer to prayer. It must be asked and received direct from God Himself. Those who know anything of the history of revivals will remember how often this has been proved—both larger and more local revivals have been distinctly traced to special prayer. In our own day there are numbers of congregations and missions where special or permanent revivals are—all glory be to God—connected with systematic, believing prayer. The coming revival will be no exception. An extraordinary spirit of prayer, urging believers to much secret and united prayer, pressing them to "labour fervently" in their supplications, will be one of the surest signs of approaching showers and floods of blessing.

Let all who are burdened with the lack of spirituality, with the low state of the life of God in believers, listen to the call that comes to all. If there is to be revival,—a mighty, Divine revival,—it will need, on our part, corresponding whole-heartedness in prayer and faith. Let not one believer think himself too weak to help, or imagine that he will not be missed. If he first begin, the gift that is in him may be so stirred that, for his circle or neighbourhood, he shall be God's chosen intercessor. Let us think of the need of souls, of all the sins and failings among God's people, of the little power there is in so much of the preaching, and begin to cry every day, "Wilt Thou not revive us again, that Thy people may rejoice in Thee?" And let us have the truth graven deep in our hearts: every revival comes, as Pentecost came, as the fruit of united, continued prayer. The coming revival must begin with a great prayer revival. It is in the closet, with the door shut, that the sound of abundance of rain will be first heard. An increase of secret prayer with ministers and members, will be the sure harbinger of blessing.

3. *"Revive Thy work, O Lord!"*—A third lesson our texts teach is that it is to the humble and contrite that the revival is promised. We want the revival to come upon the proud and the self-satisfied, to break them down and save them. God will give this, but only on the condition that those who see and feel the sin of others take their burden of confession and bear it, and that all who pray for and claim in faith God's reviving power for His Church, shall humble themselves with the confession of its sins. The need of revival always points to previous decline; and decline was always caused by sin. Humiliation and contrition have ever been the conditions of revival. In all intercession confession of man's sin and God's righteous judgment is ever an essential element.

Throughout the history of Israel we continually see this. It comes out in the reformations under the pious Kings of Judah. We hear it in the prayer of men like Ezra and Nehemiah and Daniel. In Isaiah and Jeremiah and Ezekiel, as well as in the minor prophets, it is the keynote of all the warning as of all the promise. If there be no humiliation and forsaking of sin there can be no revival or deliverance: "These men have set up their idols in their hearts. Shall I at all be inquired of by them?" "To this man will I look, even to him that is poor and of a contrite spirit, and that trembleth at My word." Amid the most gracious promises of Divine visitation there is ever this note: "Be ashamed and confounded for your ways, O House of Israel."

We find the same in the New Testament. The Sermon on the Mount promises the kingdom to the poor and them that mourn. In the Epistles to the Corinthians and Galatians the religion of man, of worldly wisdom and confidence in the flesh, is exposed and denounced; without its being confessed and forsaken, all the promises of grace and the Spirit will be vain. In the Epistles to the seven churches we find five of which He, out of whose mouth goes the sharp, two-edged sword, says, that He has something against them. In each of these the keyword of His message is—not to the unconverted, but to the Church—Repent! All the glorious promises which each of these Epistles contain, down to the last one, with its "Open the door and I will come in"; "He that overcometh shall sit with Me on My throne," are dependent on that one word—Repent!

And if there is to be a revival, not among the unsaved, but in our churches, to give a holy, spiritual membership, will not that trumpet sound need to be heard—Repent? Was it only in Israel, in the ministry of kings and prophets, that there was so much evil in God's people to be cleansed away? Was it only in the Church of the first century, that Paul and James and our Lord Himself had to speak such sharp words? Or is there not in the Church of our days an idolatry of money and talent and culture, a worldly spirit, making it unfaithful to its one only Husband and Lord, a confidence in the flesh which grieves and resists God's Holy Spirit? Is there not almost everywhere a confession of the lack of spirituality and spiritual power? Let all who long for the coming revival, and seek to hasten it by their prayers, pray this above everything, that the Lord may prepare His prophets to go before Him at His bidding: "Cry aloud and spare not, lift up thy voice like a trumpet, and show My people their transgression." Every deep revival among God's people must have its roots in a deep sense and confession of sin. Until those who would lead the Church in the path of revival bear faithful testimony against the sins of the Church, it is to be feared that it will find people unprepared. Men would fain have a revival as the outgrowth of their agencies and progress. God's way is the opposite: it is out of death, acknowledged as the desert of sin, confessed as utter helplessness, that He revives. He revives the heart of the contrite one.

4. *"Revive Thy work, O Lord!"*—There is a last thought, suggested by the text from Hosea. It is as we return *to the Lord* that revival will come; for if we had not wandered from Him, His life would be among us in power. "Come and let us return to the Lord: for He hath torn, He will heal us: He hath smitten; He will bind us up: *He will revive us,* and we shall live in His sight." As we have said, there can be no return to the Lord, where there is no sense or confession of wandering. *Let us return to the Lord* must be the keynote of the revival. Let us return, acknowledging and forsaking whatever there has been in the Church that is not entirely according to His mind and spirit. Let us return, yielding up and casting out whatever there has been in our religion or along with it of the power of God's two great enemies— confidence in the flesh or the spirit of the world. Let us return, in the acknowledgment of how undividedly God must have us, to fill us with His Spirit, and use us for the kingdom of His Son. Oh, let us return, in the surrender of a dependence and a devotion which has no measure but the absolute claim of Him who is the Lord. Let us return to the Lord with our whole heart, that He may make and keep us wholly His. He will revive us, and we shall live in His sight. Let us turn to the God of Pentecost, as Christ led His disciples to turn to Him, and the God of Pentecost will turn to us.

It is for this returning to the Lord that the great work of intercession is needed. It is here the coming revival must find its strength. Let us begin as individuals in secret to plead with God, confessing whatever we see of sin or hindrance, in ourselves or others. If there were not one other sin, surely in the lack of prayer there is matter enough for repentance and confession and returning to the Lord. Let us seek to foster the spirit of confession and supplication and intercession in those around us. Let us help to encourage and to train those who think themselves too feeble. Let us lift up our voice to proclaim the great truths. The revival must come from above; the revival must be received in faith from above and brought down by prayer; the revival comes to the humble and contrite, for them to carry to others; if we return to the Lord with our whole heart, He will revive us. On those

122

who see these truths, rests the solemn responsibility of giving themselves up to witness for them and to act them out.

And as each of us pleads for the revival throughout the Church, let us specially, at the same time, cry to God for our own neighbourhood or sphere of work. Let, with every minister and worker, there be "great searchings of heart," as to whether they are ready to give such proportion of time and strength to prayer as God would have. Let them, even as in public they are leaders of their larger or smaller circles, give themselves in secret to take their places in the front rank of the great intercession host, that must prevail with God, ere the great revival, the floods of blessing can come. Of all who speak or think of, or long for, revival, let not one hold back in this great work of honest, earnest, definite pleading: Revive Thy work, O Lord! Wilt Thou not revive us again?

Come and let us return to the Lord: He will revive us! And let us know, let us follow on to know the Lord. "*His going forth* is sure as the morning; and *He shall come unto us* as the rain, as the latter rain that watereth the earth." Amen. So be it.

# NOTES

JUST this day I have been meeting a very earnest lady missionary from India. She confesses and mourns the lack of prayer. But—in India at least—it can hardly be otherwise. You have only the morning hours, from six to eleven, for your work. Some have attempted to rise at four, and get the time they think they need, and have suffered, and had to give it up. Some have tried to take time after lunch, and been found asleep on their knees. You are not your own master, and must act with others. No one who has not been in India can understand the difficulty; sufficient time for much intercession cannot be secured.

Were it only in the heat of India the difficulty existed, one might be silent. But, alas! in the coldest winter in London, and in the moderate climate of South Africa, there is the same trouble everywhere. If once we really felt—*intercession is the most important part of our work,* the securing of God's presence and power in full measure is the essential thing, this is our first duty—our hours of work would all be made subordinate to this one thing.

May God show us all whether there indeed be an insuperable difficulty for which we are not responsible, whether it be only a mistake we are making, or a sin by which we are grieving Him and hindering His Spirit!

If we ask the question George Muller once asked of a Christian, who complained that he could not find time sufficient for the study of the Word and prayer, whether an hour less work, say four hours, with the soul dwelling in the full light of God, would not be more prosperous and effective than five hours with the depressing consciousness of unfaithfulness, and the loss of the power that could be obtained in prayer, the answer will not be difficult. The more we think of it the more we feel that when earnest, godly workers allow, against their better will, the spiritual to be crowded out by incessant occupation and the fatigue it brings, it must be because the spiritual life is not sufficiently strong in them to bid the lever stand aside till the presence of God in Christ and the power of the Spirit have been fully secured.

Let us listen to Christ saying, *"Render unto Caesar the things that are Caesar's"*—let duty and work have their place—"and unto God the things that are God's." Let the worship in the Spirit, the entire dependence and continued waiting upon God for the full experience of His presence and power every day, and the strength of Christ working in us, ever have the first place. The whole question is simply this, Is God to have the place, the love, the trust, the time for personal fellowship He claims, so that all our working shall be God working in us?

## NOTE B, Chap. 7. p. 65

LET me tell here a story that occurs in one of Dr. Boardman's works. He had been invited by a lady of good position, well known as a successful worker among her husband's dependents, to come and address them. "And then," she added, "I want to speak to you about a bit of bondage of my own." When he had addressed her meeting, and found many brought to Christ through her, he wondered what her trouble might be. She soon told him. God had blessed her work, but, alas, the enjoyment she once had had in God's word and secret prayer had been lost. And she had tried her utmost to get it back, and had failed. "Ah! that is just your mistake," he said. "How that? Ought I not to do my best to have the coldness removed?" "Tell me," he said, "were you saved by doing your best?" "Oh, no! I tried long to do that, but only found rest when I ceased trying, and trusted Christ." "And that is what you need to do now. Enter your closet at the appointed time, however dull you feel, and place yourself before your Lord. Do not try to rouse an earnestness you do not feel; but quietly say to Him that He sees how all is wrong, how helpless you are, and trust Him to bless you. He will do it; as you trust quietly, His Spirit will work."

The simple story may teach many a Christian a most blessed lesson in the life of prayer. You have accepted of Christ Jesus to make you whole, and give you strength to walk in newness of life; you have claimed the Holy Spirit to be in you the Spirit of Supplication and Intercession; but do not wonder if your feelings are not all at once changed, or if your power of prayer does not come in the way you would like. It is a life of faith. By faith we receive the Holy Spirit and all His workings. Faith regards neither sight nor feeling, but rests, even when there appears to be no power to pray, in the assurance that the Spirit is praying in us as we bow quietly before God. He that thus waits in faith, and honours the Holy Spirit, and yields himself to Him, will soon find that prayer will begin to come. And he that perseveres in the faith that through Christ and by the Spirit each prayer, however feeble, is acceptable to God, will learn the lesson that it is possible to be taught by the Spirit, and led to walk worthy of the Lord to all well pleasing.

### NOTE C, Chap. 9. p. 77

JUST yesterday again—three days after the conversation mentioned in the note to chap. 7.—I met a devoted young missionary lady from the interior. As a conversation on prayer was proceeding, she interposed unasked with the remark, "But it is really impossible to find the time to pray as we wish to." I could only answer, "Time is a quantity that accommodates itself to our will; what our hearts really consider of *first importance* in the day, we will soon succeed in finding time for." It must surely be that the ministry of intercession has never been put before our students in Theological Halls and Missionary Training Homes as the most important part of their life-work. We have thought of our work in preaching or visiting as our real duty, and of prayer as a subordinate means to do this work successfully. Would not the whole position be changed if we regarded the ministry of intercession as the chief thing—*getting the blessing and power of God for the souls entrusted to us?* Then our work would take its right place, and become the subordinate one of really dispensing blessings which we had received from God. It was when the friend at midnight, in answer to his prayer, had received from Another as much as he needed, that he could supply his hungry friend. It was the intercession, going out and importuning, that was the difficult work; returning home with his rich supply to impart was easy, joyful work. This is Christ's divine order for all thy work, my brother: First come, in utter poverty, every day, and get from God the blessing in intercession, go then rejoicingly to impart it.

### NOTE D, Chap. 10. p. 84

LET me once again refer my readers to William Law, and repeat what I have said before, that no book has so helped me to an insight into the place and work of the Holy Spirit in the economy of redemption as his ADDRESS TO THE CLERGY.[1]

[1] *The Power of the Spirit: An Address to the Clergy.* By WILLIAM LAW. With additional Extracts and an Introduction by Rev. A. M. James Nisbet & Co.

The way in which he opens up how God's one object was to dwell in man, making him partaker of His goodness and glory, other way than by Himself living and working in him, gives one the key to what Pentecost and the sending forth of the Spirit of God's Son into our hearts really means. It is Christ in God's name really regaining and retaking possession of the home He had created for Himself. It is God entering into the secret depths of our nature there to "work to will and to do," to "work that which is pleasing in His sight in Christ Jesus." It is as this truth enters into us, and we see that there is and can be no good in us but what God works, that we shall see light on the Divine mystery of prayer, and believe in the Holy Spirit as breathing within us desires which God will fulfil when we yield to them, and believingly present them in the name of Christ. We shall then see that just as wonderful and prevailing as the intercession and prayer passing from the Incarnate Son to the Father in heaven is our intercourse with God; the Spirit, who is God, breathing and praying in us amid all our feebleness His heaven-born Divine petitions: what a heavenly thing prayer becomes.

The latter part of the above-mentioned book consists of extracts from Law's letters. These have been published separately.[1] No one who will take the time quietly to read and master the so simple but deep teaching they contain, without being wonderfully strengthened in the confidence which is needed, if we are to pray much and boldly. As we learn that the Holy Spirit is within us to reveal Christ there, to make us in living reality partakers of His death, His life, His merit, His disposition, so that He is formed within us, we will begin to see how Divinely right and sure it is that our intercessions in His name must be heard; His own Spirit maintains the living union with Himself, in whom we are brought nigh to God, and gives us boldness of access; what I have so feebly said in the chapter on the Spirit of Supplication will get new meaning; and, what is more, the exercise of prayer a new attractiveness; its solemn Divine mystery will humble us, its unspeakable privilege lift us up in faith and adoration.

### NOTE E, Chap. 11. p. 91

THERE is a question, the deepest of all, on which I have not entered in this book. I have spoken of the lack of prayer in the

---

[1] *The Divine Indwelling.* Selections from the Letters of William Law. With Introduction by A. M., James Nisbet & Co.

individual Christian as a symptom of a disease. But what shall we say of it, that there is such a widespread prevalence of this failure to give a due proportion of time and strength to prayer? Do we not need to inquire, How comes it that the Church of Christ, endued with the Holy Ghost, cannot train its ministers and workers and members to place first what is first? How comes it that the confession of too little prayer, and the call for more prayer, is so frequently heard, and yet the evil continues? The Spirit of God, the Spirit of Supplication and Intercession, is in the Church and in every believer. There must surely be some other spirit of great power resisting and hindering this Spirit of God. It is indeed so. The spirit of the world, which under all its beautiful and even religious activities is the spirit of the god of this world, is the great hindrance. Everything that is done on earth, whether within or without the Church, is done by either of these two spirits. What is in the individual the flesh, is in mankind as a whole the spirit of the world; and all the power the flesh has in the individual is owing to the place given to the spirit of this world in the Church and in Christian life. It is the spirit of the world is the great hindrance to the spirit of prayer. All our most earnest calls to men to pray more will be vain except this evil be acknowledged and combated and overcome. The believer and the Church must be entirely freed from the spirit of the world.

And how is this to be done? There is but one way—the Cross of Christ, "by which," as Paul says, "the world is crucified unto me, and I unto the world." It is only through death to the world that we can be freed from its spirit. The separation must be vital and entire. It is only through the acceptance of our crucifixion with Christ that we can live out this confession, and, as crucified to the world, maintain the position of irreconcilable hostility to whatever is of its spirit and not of the Spirit of God; and it is only God Himself who, by His Divine power, can lead us into and keep us daily dead to sin, and alive unto God in Christ Jesus. The cross, with its shame and its separation from the world, and its death to all that is of flesh and of self, is the only power that can conquer the spirit of the world.

I have felt so strongly that the truth needs to be anew asserted, that I hope, if it please God, to publish a volume, *The Cross of Christ*, with the inquiry into what God's word teaches as to our actual participation with Christ in His crucifixion. Christ prayed on the way to the cross. He prayed Himself to the cross. He prayed on the cross. He prays ever as the fruit of the cross. As the Church lives on the cross, and the cross lives in the Church, the spirit of prayer will be given. In Christ it was the crucifixion spirit and death that was the source of the Intercession Spirit and Power. With us it can be no otherwise.

NOTE F, Chap. 14. p. 115

I HAVE more than once spoken of the need of training Christians to the work of intercession. In a previous note I have asked the question whether, in the teaching of our Theological Halls and Mission Training Houses, sufficient attention is given to prayer as the most important, and in some senses the most difficult part of the work for which the students are being prepared. I have wondered whether it might not be possible to offer those who are willing, during their student life, to put themselves under a course of training, some help in the way of hints and suggestions as to what is needed to give prayer the place and the power in our ministry it ought to have.

As a rule, it is in the student life that the character must be formed for future years, and it is in the present student world that the Church of the future must be influenced. If God allows me to carry out a plan that is hardly quite mature yet, I would wish to publish a volume, THE STUDENT'S PRAYER MANUAL, combining the teaching of Scripture as to what is most needed to make men of prayer of us, with such practical directions as may help a young Christian, preparing to devote his life to God's service successfully, to cultivate such a spirit and habit of prayer as shall abide with him through all his coming life and labours.

# HELPS TO INTERCESSION

PRAYING ALWAYS
WITH ALL PRAYER AND SUPPLICATION
IN THE SPIRIT
AND WATCHING THEREUNTO WITH ALL PERSEVERANCE
AND SUPPLICATION FOR ALL SAINTS
AND FOR ME

I EXHORT THAT FIRST OF ALL
SUPPLICATION, PRAYERS, INTERCESSIONS
GIVING OF THANKS
BE MADE FOR ALL MEN
FOR KINGS, AND ALL THAT ARE IN AUTHORITY

PRAY FOR ONE ANOTHER

## HELPS TO INTERCESSION

Pray without Ceasing.—Who can do this? How can one do it who is surrounded by the cares of daily life?—How can a mother love her child without ceasing? How can the eyelid without ceasing hold itself ready to protect the eye? How can I breathe and feel and hear without ceasing? Because all these are the functions of a healthy, natural life. And so, if the spiritual life be healthy, under the full power of the Holy Spirit, praying without ceasing will be natural.

Pray without Ceasing—Does it refer to continual acts of prayer, in which we are to persevere till we obtain, or to the spirit of prayerfulness that should animate us all the day? It includes both. The example of our Lord Jesus shows us this. We have to enter our closet for special seasons of prayer; we are at times to persevere there in importunate prayer. We are also all the day to walk in God's presence, with the whole heart set upon heavenly things. Without set times of prayer the spirit of prayer will be dull and feeble. Without the continual prayerfulness the set times will not avail.

Pray without Ceasing.—Does that refer to prayer for ourselves or others? To both. It is because many confine it to themselves that they fail so in practising it. It is only when the branch gives itself to bear fruit, more fruit, much fruit, that it can live a healthy life, and expect a rich inflow of sap. The death of Christ brought Him to the place of everlasting intercession. Your death with Him to sin and self sets you free from the care of self, and elevates you to the dignity of intercessor—one who can get life and blessing from God for others. Know your calling; begin this your work. Give yourself wholly to it, and ere you know you will be finding something of this "*Praying always*" within you.

Pray without Ceasing.—How can I learn it? The best way of learning to do a thing—in fact the only way—is *to do it*. Begin by setting apart some time every day, say ten or fifteen minutes, in which you say to God and to yourself, that you come to Him now as intercessor for others. Let it be after your morning or evening prayer, or any other time. If you cannot secure the same time every day, be not troubled. Only see that you do your work. Christ chose you and appointed you to pray for others.

If at first you do not feel any special urgency or faith or power in your prayers, let not that hinder you. Quietly tell your Lord Jesus of your feebleness; believe that the Holy Spirit is in you to teach you to pray, and be assured that if you begin, God will help you. God cannot help you unless you begin and keep on.

Pray without Ceasing.—How do I know what to pray for? If once you begin, and think of all the needs around you, you will soon find enough. But to help you this little tract is issued, with subjects and hints for prayer for a month. It is meant that we should use it month by month, until we know more fully to follow the Spirit's leading, and have learnt, if need be, to make our own list of subjects, and can dispense with it. In regard to the use of these helps a few words may be needed.

How to Pray.—You notice for every day two headings—the one What to Pray; the other, How to Pray. If the subjects were only given, one might fall into the routine of mentioning names and things before God, and the work become a burden. The hints under the heading How to Pray are meant to remind of the spiritual nature of the work, of the need of Divine help, and to encourage faith in the certainty that God, through the Spirit, will give us grace to pray aright, and will also hear our prayer. One does not at once learn to take his place boldly, and to dare to believe that he will be heard. Therefore take a few moments each day to listen to God's voice reminding you of how certainly even you will be heard, and calling on you to pray in that faith in your Father, to claim and take the blessing you plead for. And let these words about How to Pray enter your hearts and occupy your thoughts at other times too. The work of intercession is Christ's great work on earth, intrusted to Him because He gave Himself a sacrifice to God for men. The work of intercession is the greatest work a Christian can do. Give yourself a sacrifice to God for men, and the work will become your glory and your joy too.

What to Pray.—Scripture calls us to pray for many things: for all saints; for all men; for kings and all rulers; for all who are in adversity; for the sending forth of labourers; for those who labour in the gospel; for all converts; for believers who have fallen into sin; for one another in our own immediate circles. The Church is now so much larger than when the New Testament was written; the number of forms of work and workers is so much greater; the needs of the Church and the world are so much better known, that we need to take time and thought to see where prayer is needed, and to what our heart is most drawn out. The Scripture calls to prayer demand a large heart, taking in all saints, and all men, and all needs. An attempt has been made in these

134

helps to indicate what the chief subjects are that need prayer, and that ought to interest every Christian.

It will be felt difficult by many to pray for such large spheres as are sometimes mentioned. Let it be understood that in each case we may make special intercession for our own circle of interest coming under that heading. And it is hardly needful to say, further, that where one subject appears of more special interest or urgency than another we are free for a time day after day to take up that subject. If only time be really given to intercession, and the spirit of believing intercession be cultivated, the object is attained. While, on the one hand, the heart must be enlarged at times to take in all, the more pointed and definite our prayer can be the better.

Answers to Prayer.—More than one little book has been published in which Christians may keep a register of their petitions, and note when they were answered, so that petitions regarding individual souls or special spheres of work may be recorded, and the answer looked for.[1] When we pray for all saints, or for missions in general, it is difficult to know when or how our prayer is answered, or whether our prayer has had any part in bringing the answer. It is of extreme importance that we should prove that God hears us, and to this end take note of what answers we look for, and when they come. On the day of praying for all saints, take the saints in your congregation, or in your prayer-meeting, and ask for a revival among them. Take, in connection with missions, some special station or missionary you are interested in, or more than one, and plead for blessing. And expect and look for its coming, that you may praise God.

Prayer Circles.—There is no desire in publishing this invitation to intercession to add another to the many existing prayer unions or praying bands. The first object is to stir the many Christians who practically, through ignorance of their calling, or unbelief as to their prayer availing much, take but very little part in the work of intercession; and then to help those who do pray to some fuller apprehension of the greatness of the work, and the need of giving their whole strength to it. There is a circle of prayer which asks for prayer on the first day of every month for the fuller manifestation of the power of the Holy Spirit throughout the Church. I have given the words of that invitation as subject for the first day, and taken the same thought as keynote all through. The more one thinks of the need and the promise, and the greatness of the obstacles to be overcome in prayer, the more one feels it must

[1] Such as: *Daily* by C. F. Harford, Marshall, Morgan & Scott.

135

become our life work day by day, that to which every other interest is subordinated.

But while not forming a large prayer union, it is suggested that it may be found helpful to have small prayer circles to unite in prayer, either for one month, with some special object introduced daily along with the others, or through a year or longer, with the view of strengthening each other in the grace of intercession. If a minister were to invite some of his neighbouring brethren to join for some special requests along with the printed subjects for supplication, or a number of the more earnest members of his congregagation to unite in prayer for revival, some might be trained to take their place in the great work of intercession, who now stand idle because no man hath hired them.

Who is sufficient for these things?—The more we study and try to practise this grace of intercession, the more we become overwhelmed by its greatness and our feebleness. Let every such impression lead us to listen: My grace is sufficient for thee, and to answer truthfully: Our sufficiency is of God. Take courage; it is in the intercession of Christ you are called to take part. The burden and the agony, the triumph and the victory are all His. Learn from Him, yield to His Spirit in you, to know how to pray. He gave Himself a sacrifice to God for men, that He might have the right and power of intercession. "He bare the sin of many, and made intercession for the transgressors." Let your faith rest boldly on His finished work. Let your heart wholly identify itself with Him in His death and His life. Like Him, give yourself to God a sacrifice for men: it is your highest nobility, it is your true and full union to Him; it will be to you, as to Him, your power of intercession. Beloved Christian! come and give your whole heart and life to intercession, and you will know its blessedness and its power. God asks nothing less; the world needs nothing less; Christ asks nothing less; let nothing less be what we offer to God.

### WHAT TO PRAY—*For the Power of the Holy Spirit*

"I bow my knees unto the Father, that He would grant you that ye may be strengthened with power through His Spirit."—Eph. 3:16.

"Wait for the promise of the Father."—Acts 1:4.

"The fuller manifestation of the grace and energy of the Blessed Spirit of God, in the removal of all that is contrary to God's revealed will, so that we grieve not the Holy Spirit, but that He may work in mightier power in the Church, for the exaltation of Christ and the blessing of souls."

God has one promise to and through His exalted Son; our Lord has one gift to His Church; the Church has one need; all prayer unites in the one petition—the power of the Holy Spirit. Make it your one prayer.

### HOW TO PRAY—*As a Child asks a Father*

"If a son ask bread of any of you that is a father, will he give him a stone? How much more shall your Heavenly Father give the Holy Spirit to them that ask Him?"—Luke 11:11, 13.

Ask as simply and trustfully as a child asks bread. You can do this because "God has sent forth the Spirit of His Son into your heart, crying, Abba, Father." This Spirit is in you to give you childlike confidence. In the faith of His praying in you, ask for the power of that Holy Spirit everywhere. Mention places or circles where you specially ask it to be seen.

### WHAT TO PRAY—*For the Spirit of Supplication*

"The Spirit Himself maketh intercession for us."—Rom. 8:26.

"I will pour out the Spirit of Supplication."—Zech. 12:10.

"The evangelisation of the world depends first of all upon a revival of prayer. Deeper than the need for men—ay, deep down at the bottom of our spiritless life—is the need for the forgotten secret of prevailing, world-wide prayer."

Every child of God has the Holy Spirit in him to pray. God waits to give the Spirit in full measure. Ask for yourself, and all who join, the outpouring of the Spirit of Supplication. Ask it for your own prayer circle.

"With all prayer and supplication, praying at all seasons in the Spirit."—Eph. 6:18.

"Praying in the Holy Spirit."—Jude 20.

Our Lord gave His disciples on His resurrection day the Holy Spirit to enable them to wait for the full outpouring on the day of Pentecost. It is only in the power of the Spirit already in us, acknowledged and yielded to, that we can pray for His fuller manifestation. Say to the Father, it is the Spirit of His Son in you is urging you to plead His promise.

### THIRD DAY

### WHAT TO PRAY—*For all Saints*

"With all prayer and supplication praying at all seasons, and watching thereunto in all perseverance and supplication for all saints."—Eph. 6:18.

Every member of a body is interested in the welfare of the whole, and exists to help and complete the others. Believers are one body, and ought to pray, not so much for the welfare of their own church or society, but, first of all, for all saints. This large, unselfish love is the proof that Christ's Spirit and Love is teaching them to pray. Pray first for all and then for the believers around you.

### HOW TO PRAY—*In the Love of the Spirit*

"By this shall all men know that ye are My disciples, if ye have love one to another."—John 13:35.

"I pray that they all may be one, that the world may believe that Thou didst send Me."—John 17:21.

"I beseech you, brethren, by the love of the Spirit, that ye strive together with me in your prayers to God for me."—Rom. 15:30.

"Above all things being fervent in your love among your selves."—1 Pet. 4:8.

If we are to pray we must love. Let us say to God we do love all His saints; let us say we love specially every child of His we know. Let us pray with fervent love, in the love of the Spirit.

## WHAT TO PRAY—*For the Spirit of Holiness*

God is the Holy One. His people is a holy people. He speaks: I am holy: I am the Lord which make you holy. Christ prayed: Sanctify them. Make them holy through Thy Truth. Paul prayed: "God establish your hearts unblamable in holiness." "God sanctify you wholly!"

Pray for all saints—God's holy ones—throughout the Church, that the Spirit of holiness may rule them. Specially for new converts. For the saints in your own neighbourhood or congregation. For any you are specially interested in. Think of their special need, weakness, or sin, and pray that God may make them holy.

## HOW TO PRAY—*Trusting in God's Omnipotence*

The things that are impossible with men are possible with God. When we think of the great things we ask for, of how little likelihood there is of their coming, of our own insignificance. Prayer is not only wishing, or asking, but believing and accepting. Be still before God and ask Him to give you to know Him as the Almighty One, and leave your petitions with Him who doeth wonders.

## WHAT TO PRAY—*That God's People may be kept from the World*

"Holy Father, keep through Thine own name those whom Thou hast given Me. I pray not that Thou shouldest take them out of the world, but that Thou shouldest keep them from the evil. They are not of the world, as I am not of the world."—John 17:11, 15, 16.

In the last night Christ asked three things for His disciples: that they might be kept as those who are not of the world; that they might be sanctified; that they might be one in love. You cannot do better than pray as Jesus prayed. Ask for God's people that they may be kept separate from the world and its spirit; that they, by the Holy Spirit, may live as those who are not of the world.

## HOW TO PRAY—*Having Confidence before God*

"Beloved, if our hearts condemn us not, then have we confidence toward God. And whatsoever we ask, we receive of Him, because we keep His commandments, and do those things that are pleasing in His sight."—1 John 3:21, 22.

Learn these words by heart. Get them into your heart. Join the ranks of those who, with John, draw nigh to God with an assured heart, that does not condemn them, having confidence toward God. In this spirit pray for your brother who sins (1 John 5:16). In the quiet confidence of an obedient child plead for those of your brethren who may be giving way to sin. Pray for all to be kept from the evil. And say often, "What we ask, we receive, because we keep and do."

### SIXTH DAY

### WHAT TO PRAY—*For the Spirit of Love in the Church*

"I pray that they may be one, even as we are one: I in them and Thou in Me; that the world may know that Thou didst send Me, and hast loved them as Thou hast loved Me ... that the love wherewith Thou hast loved Me may be in them, and I in them."—John 17:23.

"The fruit of the Spirit is love."—Gal. 5:22.

Believers are one in Christ, as He is one with the Father. The love of God rests on them, and can dwell in them. Pray that the power of the Holy Ghost may so work this love in believers, that the world may see and know God's love in them. Pray much for this.

### HOW TO PRAY—*As one of God's Remembrancers*

"I have set watchmen on thy walls, which shall never hold their peace day nor night: ye that are the Lord's remembrancers, keep not silence, and give Him no rest."—Isa. 62:6.

Study these words until your whole soul be filled with the consciousness, I am appointed intercessor. Enter God's presence in that faith. Study the world's need with that thought—it is my work to intercede; the Holy Spirit will teach me for what and how. Let it be an abiding consciousness: My great life-work, like Christ's, is intercession—to pray for believers and those who do not yet know God.

140

## WHAT TO PRAY—*For the Power of the Holy Spirit on Ministers*

"I beseech you that ye strive together with me in your prayers to God for me."—Rom. 15:30.

"He will deliver us; ye also helping together by your supplication on our behalf."—2 Cor. 1:10, 11.

What a great host of ministers there are in Christ's Church. What need they have of prayer. What a power they might be, if they were all clothed with the power of the Holy Ghost. Pray definitely for this; long for it. Think of your own minister, and ask it very specially for him. Connect every thought of the ministry, in your town or neighbourhood or the world, with the prayer that all may be filled with the Spirit. Plead for them the promise, "Tarry till ye be clothed with power from on high." "Ye shall receive power, when the Holy Ghost is come upon you."

## HOW TO PRAY—*In Secret*

"But thou, when thou prayest, enter into thy inner chamber, and having shut to thy door, pray to the Father which is in secret."—Matt. 6:6.

"He withdrew again into the mountain to pray, *Himself alone.*"—Matt. 14:23; John 6:15.

Take time and realise, when you are alone with God: Here am I now, face to face with God, to intercede for His servants. Do not think you have no influence, or that your prayer will not be missed. Your prayer and faith will make a difference. Cry in secret to God for His ministers.

## EIGHTH DAY

## WHAT TO PRAY—*For the Spirit on all Christian Workers*

"Ye also helping together on our behalf; that for the gift bestowed upon us by means of many, thanks may be given by many on our behalf."—2 Cor. 1:11.

What multitudes of workers in connection with our churches and missions, our railways and postmen, our soldiers and sailors, our young men and young women, our fallen men and women,

141

our poor and sick. God be praised for this! What could they accomplish if each were living in the fulness of the Holy Spirit? Pray for them; it makes you a partner in their work, and you will praise God each time you hear of blessing anywhere.

### HOW TO PRAY—*With definite Petitions*

"What wilt thou that I should do unto thee?"—Luke 18:41.

The Lord knew what the man wanted, and yet He asked him. The utterance of our wish gives point to the transaction in which we are engaged with God, and so awakens faith and expectation. Be very definite in your petitions, so as to know what answer you may look for. Just think of the great host of workers, and ask and expect God definitely to bless them in answer to the prayers of His people. Then ask still more definitely for workers around you. Intercession is not the breathing out of pious wishes; its aim is, in believing, persevering prayer, to receive and bring down blessing.

### NINTH DAY

### WHAT TO PRAY—*For God's Spirit on our Mission Work*

"The evangelisation of the world depends first of all upon a revival of prayer. Deeper than the need for men—ay, deep down at the bottom of our spiritless life, is the need for the forgotten secret of prevailing, world-wide prayer."

"As they ministered to the Lord, and fasted, the Holy Ghost said, Separate Me Barnabas and Saul. Then when they had fasted and prayed, they sent them away. So they, being sent forth by the Holy Ghost, departed."—Acts 13:2, 3, 4.

Pray that our mission work may all be done in this spirit— waiting on God, hearing the voice of the Spirit, sending forth men with fasting and prayer. Pray that in our churches our mission interest and mission work may be in the power of the Holy Spirit and of prayer. It is a Spirit-filled, praying Church will send out Spirit-filled missionaries, mighty in prayer.

### HOW TO PRAY—*Take Time*

"I give myself unto prayer."—Ps. 109:4.

"We will give ourselves continually to prayer."—Acts 6:4.

"Be not rash with thy mouth, and let not thine heart be hasty to utter anything before God."—Eccles. 5:2.

"And He continued all night in prayer to God."—Luke 6:12.

Time is one of the chief standards of value. The time we give is a proof of the interest we feel.

We need time with God—to realise His presence; to wait for Him to make Himself known; to consider and feel the needs we plead for; to take our place in Christ; to pray till we can believe that we have received. Take time in prayer, and pray down blessing on the mission work of the Church.

TENTH DAY

### WHAT TO PRAY—*For God's Spirit on our Missionaries*

"What the world needs to-day, is, not only more missionaries, but the outpouring of God's Spirit on everyone whom He has sent out to work for Him in the foreign field."

"Ye shall receive power, when the Holy Ghost is come upon you: and ye shall be My witnesses unto the uttermost parts of the earth."—Acts 1:8.

God always gives His servants power equal to the work He asks of them. Think of the greatness and difficulty of this work,—casting out Satan out of his strongholds,—and pray that everyone who takes part in it may receive and do all his work in the power of the Holy Ghost. Think of the difficulties of your missionaries, and pray for them.

### HOW TO PRAY—*Trusting God's Faithfulness*

"He is faithful that promised." "She counted Him faithful who promised."—Heb. 10:23, 11:11.

Just think of God's promises to His Son, concerning His kingdom; to the Church, concerning the heathen; to His servants, concerning their work; to yourself, concerning your prayer; and pray in the assurance that He is faithful, and only waits for prayer and faith to fulfil them. "Faithful is He that calleth you" (to pray), "who also will do it" (what He has promised.)

Take up individual missionaries, make yourself one with them, and pray till you know that you are heard. Oh, begin to live for Christ's kingdom as the one thing worth living for!

## WHAT TO PRAY—*For more Labourers*

"Pray ye the Lord of the harvest, that He send forth labourers into His harvest."—Matt. 9:38.

What a remarkable call of the Lord Jesus for help from His disciples in getting the need supplied. What an honour put upon prayer. What a proof that God wants prayer and will hear it.

Pray for labourers, for all students in theological seminaries, training homes, Bible institutes, that they may not go, unless He fits them and sends them forth; that our churches may train their students to seek for the sending forth of the Holy Spirit; that all believers may hold themselves ready to be sent forth, or to pray for those who can go.

## HOW TO PRAY—*In Faith, nothing Doubting*

"Jesus saith unto them, Have faith in God. Whosoever shall say unto this mountain, Be thou removed, and be thou cast into the sea; and shall not doubt in his heart, but shall believe that what he saith shall come to pass, he shall have it."—Mark 11:22, 23.

Have faith in God! Ask Him to make Himself known to you as the faithful, mighty God, who worketh all in all; and you will be encouraged to believe that He can give suitable and sufficient labourers, however impossible this appears. But, remember, in answer to prayer and faith.

Apply this to every opening where a good worker is needed. The work is God's. He can give the right workman. But He must be asked and waited on.

## WHAT TO PRAY—*For the Spirit to convince the World of Sin*

"I will send the Comforter to you. And He, when He is come, will convict the world in respect of sin."—John 16:7, 8.

God's one desire, the one object of Christ's being manifested, is to take away sin. The first work of the Spirit on the world is conviction of sin. Without that, no deep or abiding revival, no powerful conversion. Pray for it, that the gospel may be preached in such power of the Spirit, that men may see that they have rejected and crucified Christ, and cry out, What shall we do?

Pray most earnestly for a mighty power of conviction of sin wherever the gospel is preached.

### HOW TO PRAY—*Stir up yourself to take hold of God's Strength*

"Let him take hold of My strength, that he may make peace with Me."—Isa. 27:5.

"There is none that calleth upon Thy name, that stirreth himself to take hold of Thee."—Isa. 64:7.

"Stir up the gift of God which is in thee."—2 Tim. 1:6.

First, take hold of God's strength. God is a Spirit. I cannot take hold of Him, and hold Him fast, but by the Spirit. Take hold of God's strength, and hold on till it has done for you what He has promised. Pray for the power of the Spirit to convict of sin.

Second, stir up yourself, the power that is in you by the Holy Spirit, to take hold. Give your whole heart and will to it, and say, I will not let Thee go except Thou bless me.

### THIRTEENTH DAY

### WHAT TO PRAY—*For the Spirit of Burning*

"And it shall come to pass, that he that is left in Zion shall be called holy: when the Lord shall have washed away the filth of the daughters of Zion, by the spirit of judgment and the spirit of burning."—Isa. 4:3, 4.

A washing by fire! a cleansing by judgment! He that has passed through this shall be called holy. The power of blessing for the world, the power of work and intercession that will avail, depends upon the spiritual state of the Church; and that can only rise higher as sin is discovered and put away. Judgment must begin at the house of God. There must be conviction of sin for sanctification. Beseech God to give His Spirit as a spirit of judgment and a spirit of burning—to discover and burn out sin in His people.

### HOW TO PRAY—*In the Name of Christ*

"Whatsoever ye shall ask in My name, that will I do. If ye shall ask Me anything in My name, that will I do."—John 14:13, 14.

Ask in the name of your Redeemer God, who sits upon the throne. Ask what He has promised, what He gave His blood for, that sin may be put away from among His people. Ask—the prayer is after His own heart—for the spirit of deep conviction of sin to come among His people. Ask for the spirit of burning. Ask in the faith of His name—the faith of what He wills, of what He can do—and look for the answer. Pray that the Church may be blessed, to be made a blessing in the world.

FOURTEENTH DAY

### WHAT TO PRAY—*For the Church of the Future*

"That the children might not be as their fathers, a generation that set not their heart aright, and whose spirit was not steadfast with God."—Ps. 78:8.

"I will pour My Spirit upon thy seed, and My blessing upon thy offspring."—Isa. 44:3.

Pray for the rising generation, who are to come after us. Think of the young men and young women and children of this age, and pray for all the agencies at work among them; that in associations and societies and unions, in homes and schools, Christ may be honoured, and the Holy Spirit get possession of them. Pray for the young of your own neighbourhood.

### HOW TO PRAY—*With the Whole Heart*

"The Lord grant thee according to thine own heart."—Ps. 20:4.

"Thou hast given him his heart's desire."—Ps. 21:2.

"I cried with my whole heart; hear me, O Lord."—Ps. 119:145.

God lives, and listens to every petition with His whole heart. Each time we pray the whole Infinite God is there to hear. He asks that in each prayer the whole man shall be there too; that we shall cry with our whole heart. Christ gave Himself to God for men; and so He takes up every need into His intercession. If once we seek God with our whole heart, the whole heart will be in every prayer with which we come to this God. Pray with your whole heart for the young.

## WHAT TO PRAY—*For Schools and Colleges*

"As for Me, this is My covenant with them, saith the Lord: My Spirit that is upon thee, and My words which I have put in thy mouth, shall not depart out of thy mouth, nor out of the mouth of thy seed, nor out of the mouth of thy seed's seed, saith the Lord, from henceforth and for ever."—Isa. 59:21.

The future of the Church and the world depends, to an extent we little conceive, on the education of the day. The Church may be seeking to evangelise the heathen, and be giving up her own children to secular and materialistic influences. Pray for schools and colleges, and that the Church may realise and fulfil its momentous duty of caring for its children. Pray for godly teachers.

## HOW TO PRAY—*Not Limiting God*

"They limited the Holy One of Israel."—Ps. 78:41.

"He did not many mighty works there because of their unbelief."—Matt. 13:58.

"Is anything too hard for the Lord?"—Gen. 18:14.

"Ah, Lord God! Thou hast made the heaven and the earth by Thy great power; there is nothing too hard for Thee. Behold, I am the Lord: is there anything too hard for Me?"—Jer. 32:17, 27.

Beware, in your prayer, above everything, of limiting God, not only by unbelief, but by fancying that you know what He can do. Expect unexpected things, above all that we ask or think. Each time you intercede, be quiet first and worship God in His glory. Think of what He can do, of how He delights to hear Christ, of your place in Christ, and expect great things.

## SIXTEENTH DAY

## WHAT TO PRAY—*For the Power of the Holy Spirit in our Sabbath Schools*

"Thus saith the Lord, Even the captives of the mighty shall be taken away, and the prey of the terrible shall be delivered: for I will contend with him that contendeth with thee, and I will save thy children."—Isa. 49:25.

Every part of the work of God's Church is His work. He must do it. Prayer is the confession that He will, the surrender of ourselves into His hands to let Him, work in us and through us. Pray for the hundreds of thousands of Sunday-school teachers, that those who know God may be filled with His Spirit. Pray for your own Sunday school. Pray for the salvation of the children.

### HOW TO PRAY—*Boldly*

"We have a great High Priest, Jesus the Son of God. Let us therefore come boldly unto the throne of grace."—Heb. 4:14, 16.

These hints to help us in our work of intercession—what are they doing for us? Making us conscious of our feebleness in prayer? Thank God for this. It is the very first lesson we need on the way to pray the effectual prayer that availeth much. Let us persevere, taking each subject boldly to the throne of grace. As we pray we shall learn to pray, and to believe, and to expect with increasing boldness. Hold fast your assurance: it is at God's command you come as an intercessor. Christ will give you grace to pray aright.


### SEVENTEENTH DAY

### WHAT TO PRAY—*For Kings and Rulers*

"I exhort therefore, first of all, that supplications, prayers, intercessions, thanksgiving, be made for all men; for kings, and all that are in high places; that we may lead a tranquil and quiet life in all godliness and gravity."—1 Tim. 2:1, 2.

What a faith in the power of prayer! A few feeble and despised Christians are to influence the mighty Roman emperors, and help in securing peace and quietness. Let us believe that prayer is a power that is taken up by God in His rule of the world. Let us pray for our country and its rulers; for all the rulers of the world; for rulers in cities or districts in which we are interested. When God's people unite in this, they may count upon their prayer effecting in the unseen world more than they know. Let faith hold this fast.

### HOW TO PRAY—*The Prayer before God as Incense*

"And another angel came and stood at the altar, having a golden censer; and there was given unto him much incense, that he should add it unto the prayers of all the saints upon the golden altar which was before the throne. And the smoke of the incense, with the prayers of the saints, went up before God out of the angel's hand. And the angel taketh the censer; and he filled it with the fire upon the altar, and cast it upon the earth: and there followed thunder, and voices, and lightning, and an earthquake."—Rev. 8:3-5.

The same censer brings the prayer of the saints before God and casts fire upon the earth. The prayers that go up to heaven have their share in the history of this earth. Be sure that thy prayers enter God's presence.

### WHAT TO PRAY—*For Peace*

"I exhort therefore, first of all, that supplication be made for kings and all that are in high places; that we may lead a tranquil and quiet life in all godliness and gravity. For this is good and acceptable in the sight of God our Saviour."—1 Tim. 2:1-3.

"He maketh wars to cease to the end of the earth."—Ps. 46:9.

What a terrible sight!—the military armaments in which the nations find their pride. What a terrible thought!—the evil passions that may at any moment bring on war. And what a prospect the suffering and desolation that must come. God can, in answer to the prayer of His people, give peace. Let us pray for it, and for the rule of righteousness on which alone it can be stablished.

### HOW TO PRAY—*With the Understanding*

"What is it then? I will pray with the spirit, and I will pray with the understanding."—1 Cor. 14:15.

We need to pray with the spirit, as the vehicle of the intercession of God's Spirit, if we are to take hold of God in faith and power. We need to pray with the understanding, if we are really to enter deeply into the needs we bring before Him. Take time to apprehend intelligently, in each subject, the nature, the extent, the urgency of the request, the ground and way and certainty of God's promise as revealed in His Word. Let the mind affect the heart. Pray with the understanding and with the spirit.

## WHAT TO PRAY—*For the Holy Spirit on Christendom*

"Having a form of godliness, but denying the power thereof."
—2 Tim. 3:5.

"Thou hast a name that though livest, and thou art dead."—
Rev. 3:1.

There are five hundred millions of nominal Christians. The state of the majority is unspeakably awful. Formality, worldliness, ungodliness, rejection of Christ's service, ignorance, and indifference—to what an extent does all this prevail. We pray for the heathen—oh! do let us pray for those bearing Christ's name, many in worse than heathen darkness.

Does not one feel as if one ought to begin to give up his life, and to cry day and night to God for souls? In answer to prayer God gives the power of the Holy Ghost.

## HOW TO PRAY—*In deep Stillness of Soul*

"My soul is silent unto God: from Him cometh my salvation."
—Ps. 62:1.

Prayer has its power in God alone. The nearer a man comes to God Himself, the deeper he enters into God's will; the more he takes hold of God, the more power in prayer.

God must reveal Himself. If it please Him to make Himself known, He can make the heart conscious of His presence. Our posture must be that of holy reverence, of quiet waiting and adoration.

As your month of intercession passes on, and you feel the greatness of your work, be still before God. Thus you will get power to pray.

## WHAT TO PRAY—*For God's Spirit on the Heathen*

"Behold, these shall come from far; and these from the land of Sinim."—Isa. 49:12.

"Princes shall come out of Egypt; Ethiopia shall haste to stretch out her hands to God."—Ps. 68:31.

"I the Lord will hasten it in His time."—Isa. 60:22.

Pray for the heathen, who are yet without the word. Think of China, with her three hundred millions—a million a month dying without Christ. Think of Dark Africa, with its two hundred millions. Think of thirty millions a year going down into the thick darkness. If Christ gave His life for them, will you not do so? You can give yourself up to intercede for them. Just begin, if you have never yet begun, with this simple monthly school of intercession. The ten minutes you give will make you feel this is not enough. God's Spirit will draw you on. Persevere, however feeble you are. Ask God to give you some country or tribe to pray for. Can anything be nobler than to do as Christ did? Give your life for the heathen.

### HOW TO PRAY—*With Confident Expectation of an Answer*

"Call unto Me, and I will answer thee, and will shew thee great things and difficult, which thou knowest not."—Jer. 33:3.

"Thus saith the Lord God: I will yet be inquired of, that I do it."—Ezek. 36:37.

Both texts refer to promises definitely made, but their fulfilment would depend upon prayer: God would be inquired of to do it.

Pray for God's fulfilment of His promises to His Son and His Church, and expect the answer. Plead for the heathen: plead God's promises.


### TWENTY-FIRST DAY

### WHAT TO PRAY—*For God's Spirit on the Jews*

"I will pour out upon the house of David, and the inhabitants of Jerusalem, the Spirit of grace and Supplication; and they shall look unto Me whom they pierced."—Zech. 12:10.

"Brethren, my heart's desire and my supplication to God is for them, that they may be saved."—Rom. 10:1.

Pray for the Jews. Their return to the God of their fathers stands connected, in a way we cannot tell, with wonderful blessing to the Church, and with the coming of our Lord Jesus. Let us not think that God has foreordained all this, and that we cannot hasten it. In a divine and mysterious way God has connected His fulfilment of His promise with our prayer. His Spirit's intercession in us is God's forerunner of blessing. Pray for Israel and the work done among them. And pray too: Amen. Even so, come, Lord Jesus!

### HOW TO PRAY—*With the Intercession of the Holy Spirit*

"We know not how to pray as we ought; but the Spirit Himself maketh intercession for us with groanings which cannot be uttered."—Rom. 8:26.

In your ignorance and feebleness believe in the secret indwelling and intercession of the Holy Spirit within you. Yield yourself to His life and leading habitually. He will help your infirmities in prayer. Plead the promises of God even where you do not see how they are to be fulfilled. God knows the mind of the Spirit, because He maketh intercession for the saints according to the will of God. Pray with the simplicity of a little child; pray with the holy awe and reverence of one in whom God's Spirit dwells and prays.

### TWENTY-SECOND DAY

### WHAT TO PRAY—*For all who are in Suffering*

"Remember them that are in bonds, as bound with them; them that are evil entreated, as being yourselves in the body."—Heb. 13:3.

What a world of suffering we live in! How Jesus sacrificed all and identified Himself with it! Let us in our measure do so too. The persecuted Stundists and Armenians and Jews, the famine-stricken millions of India, the hidden slavery of Africa, the poverty and wretchedness of our great cities—and so much more: what suffering among those who know God and who know Him not. And then in smaller circles in ten thousand homes and hearts, what sorrow. In our own neighbourhood, how many needing help or comfort. Let us have a heart for, let us think of the suffering. It will stir us to pray, to work, to hope, to love more. And in a way and time we know not God will hear our prayer.

### HOW TO PRAY—*Praying always, and not fainting*

"He spake unto them a parable to the end that they ought always to pray, and not to faint."—Luke 18:1.

Do you not begin to feel prayer is really the help for this sinful world? What a need there is of unceasing prayer? The very greatness of the task makes us despair! What can our ten minutes of intercession avail? It is right we feel this: this is the way in which God is calling and preparing us to give our life to prayer. Give yourself wholly to God for men, and amid all your work, your heart will be drawn out to men in love, and drawn up to

God in dependence and expectation. To a heart thus led by the Holy Spirit, it is possible to pray always and not to faint.

## WHAT TO PRAY—*For the Holy Spirit in your own Work*

"I labour, striving according to His working, which worketh in me mightily."—Col. 1:29.

You have your own special work; make it a work of intercession. Paul laboured, striving according to the working of God in him. Remember, God is not only the Creator, but the Great Workman, who worketh all in all. You can only do your work in His strength, by Him working in you through the Spirit. Intercede much for those among whom you work, till God gives you life for them.

Let us all intercede too for each other, for every worker throughout God's Church, however solitary or unknown.

## HOW TO PRAY—*In God's very Presence*

"Draw nigh to God, and He will draw nigh to you."—Jas. 4:8.

The nearness of God gives rest and power in prayer. The nearness of God is given to him who makes it his first object. "Draw nigh to God"; seek the nearness to Him, and He will give it; "He will draw nigh to you." Then it becomes easy to pray in faith.

Remember that when first God takes you into the school of intercession it is almost more for your own sake than that of others. You have to be trained to love, and wait, and pray, and believe. Only persevere. Learn to set yourself in His presence, to wait quietly for the assurance that He draws nigh. Enter His holy presence, tarry there, and spread your work before Him. Intercede for the souls you are working among. Get a blessing from God, His Spirit into your own heart, for them.

## WHAT TO PRAY—*For the Spirit on your own Congregation*

"Beginning at Jerusalem."—Luke 24:47.

Each one of us is connected with some congregation or circle of believers, who are to us the part of Christ's body with which we come into most direct contact. They have a special claim on our intercession. Let it be a settled matter between God and you that you are to labour in prayer on its behalf. Pray for the minister and all leaders or workers in it. Pray for the believers according to their needs. Pray for conversions. Pray for the power of the Spirit to manifest itself. Band yourself with others to join in secret in definite petitions. Let intercession be a definite work, carried on as systematically as preaching or Sunday school. And pray, expecting an answer.

### HOW TO PRAY—*Continually*

"Watchmen, that shall never hold their peace day nor night."
—Isa. 62:6.

"His own elect, that cry to Him day and night."—Luke 18:7.

"Night and day praying exceedingly, that we may perfect that which is lacking in your faith."—1 Thess. 3:10.

"A widow indeed, hath her hope set in God, and continueth in supplications night and day."—1 Tim. 5:5.

When the glory of God, and the love of Christ, and the need of souls are revealed to us, the fire of this unceasing intercession will begin to burn in us for those who are near and those who are far off.

#### TWENTY-FIFTH DAY

### WHAT TO PRAY—*For more Conversions*

"He is able to save completely, seeing He ever liveth to make intercession."—Heb. 7:25.

"We will give ourselves continually to prayer and the ministry of the word.... And the word of God increased; and the number of the disciples multiplied exceedingly."—Acts 6:4, 7.

Christ's power to save, and save completely, depends on His unceasing intercession. The apostles withdrawing themselves from other work to give themselves continually to prayer was followed by the number of the disciples multiplying exceedingly. As we, in our day, give ourselves to intercession, we shall have more and mightier conversions. Let us plead for this. Christ is exalted to give repentance. The Church exists with the Divine purpose and promise of having conversions. Let us not be ashamed to confess our sin and feebleness, and cry to God for more conversions in Christian and heathen lands, of those too whom you know and love. Plead for the salvation of sinners.

### HOW TO PRAY—*In deep Humility*

"Truth, Lord: yet the dogs eat of the crumbs.... O woman,
154

great is thy faith: be it unto thee even as thou wilt."—Matt. 15:27, 28.

You feel unworthy and unable to pray aright. To accept this heartily, and to be content still to come and be blest in your unworthiness, is true humility. It proves its integrity by not seeking for anything, but simply trusting His grace. And so it is the very strength of a great faith, and gets a full answer. "Yet the dogs" —let that be your plea as you persevere for someone possibly possessed of the devil. Let not your littleness hinder you for a moment.

<br>

### TWENTY-SIXTH DAY

#### WHAT TO PRAY—*For the Holy Spirit on Young Converts*

"Peter and John prayed for them, that they might receive the Holy Ghost; for as yet He was fallen upon none of them: only they had been baptized into the name of the Lord Jesus."—Acts 8:15, 16.

"Now He which establisheth us with you in Christ, and anointed us, is God; who also gave us the earnest of the Spirit in our hearts."—2 Cor. 1:21, 22.

How many new converts who remain feeble; how many who fall into sin; how many who backslide entirely. If we pray for the Church, its growth in holiness and devotion to God's service, pray specially for the young converts. How many stand alone, surrounded by temptation; how many have no teaching on the Spirit in them, and the power of God to establish them; how many in heathen lands, surrounded by Satan's power. If you pray for the power of the Spirit in the Church, pray specially that every young convert may know that he may claim and receive the fulness of the Spirit.

#### HOW TO PRAY—*Without Ceasing*

"As for me, God forbid that I should sin against the Lord in ceasing to pray for you."—1 Sam. 12:23.

It is sin against the Lord to cease praying for others. When once we begin to see how absolutely indispensable intercession is, just as much a duty as loving God or believing in Christ, and how we are called and bound to it as believers, we shall feel that to cease intercession is grievous sin. Let us ask for grace to take up our place as priests with joy, and give our life to bring down the blessing of heaven.

155

## WHAT TO PRAY—*That God's People may Realise their Calling*

"I will bless thee; and be thou a blessing: *In thee* shall *all the families of the earth* be blessed."—Gen. 12:2, 3.

"God be merciful *unto us*, and bless *us*; and cause His face to shine *upon us*. That Thy way may be known *upon earth*, Thy saving health *among all nations*."—Ps. 67:1, 2.

Abraham was only blessed that he might be a blessing to all the earth. Israel prays for blessing, that God may be known among all nations. Every believer, just as much as Abraham, is only blessed that he may carry God's blessing to the world.

Cry to God that His people may know this, that every believer is only to live for the interests of God and His kingdom. If this truth were preached and believed and practised, what a revolution it would bring in our mission work. What a host of willing intercessors we should have. Plead with God to work it by the Holy Spirit.

### HOW TO PRAY—*As One who has Accepted for Himself what he Asks for Others*

"Peter said, What I have, I give unto thee.... The Holy Ghost fell on them, as on us at the beginning.... God gave them the like gift, as He gave unto us."—Acts 3:6, 11:15, 17.

As you pray for this great blessing on God's people, the Holy Spirit taking entire possession of them for God's service, yield yourself to God, and claim the gift anew in faith. Let each thought of feebleness or shortcoming only make you the more urgent in prayer for others; as the blessing comes to them, you too will be helped. With every prayer for conversions or mission work, pray that God's people may know how wholly they belong to Him.

### WHAT TO PRAY—*That all God's People may know the Holy Spirit*

"The Spirit of truth, whom the world knoweth not; but ye know Him; for He abideth with you, and shall be in you."—John 14:17.

"Know ye not that your body is a temple of the Holy Ghost?" —1 Cor. 6:19.

The Holy Spirit is the power of God for the salvation of men. He only works as He dwells in the Church. He is given to enable believers to live wholly as God would have them live, in the full experience and witness of Him who saves completely. Pray God that every one of His people may know the Holy Spirit!— That He, in all His fulness, is given to them! That they cannot expect to live as their Father would have, without having Him in His fulness, without being filled with Him! Pray that all God's people, even away in churches gathered out of heathendom, may learn to say: I believe in the Holy Ghost.

### HOW TO PRAY—*Labouring fervently in Prayer*

"Epaphras, who is one of you, saluteth you, always labouring fervently for you in prayers, that ye may stand perfect and complete in all the will of God."—Col. 4:12.

To a healthy man labour is a delight; in what interests him he labours fervently. The believer who is in full health, whose heart is filled with God's Spirit, labours fervently in prayer. For what? That his brethren may stand perfect and complete in all the will of God; that they may know what God wills for them, how He calls them to live, and be led and walk by the Holy Ghost. Labour fervently in prayer that all God's children may know this, as possible, as divinely sure.

### TWENTY-NINTH DAY

### WHAT TO PRAY—*For the Spirit of Intercession*

"I chose you, and appointed you, that ye should go and bear fruit; that whatsoever ye shall ask of the Father in My name, He may give it you."—John 15:16.

"Hitherto ye have asked nothing in My name. In that day ye shall ask in My name."—John 16:24, 26.

Has not our school of intercession taught us how little we have prayed in the name of Jesus? He promised His disciples: In that day, when the Holy Spirit comes upon you, ye shall ask in My name. Are there not tens of thousands with us mourning the lack of the power of intercession? Let our intercession to-day be for them and all God's children, that Christ may teach us that the Holy Spirit in us; and what it is to live in His fullness, and to yield ourselves to His intercession work within us. The Church

157

and the world need nothing so much as a mighty Spirit of Intercession to bring down the power of God on earth. Pray for the descent from heaven of the Spirit of Intercession for a great prayer revival.

### HOW TO PRAY—*Abiding in Christ*

"If ye abide in Me, and My words abide in you, ask whatsoever ye will, and it shall be done to you."—John 15:7.

Our acceptance with God, our access to Him, is all in Christ. As we consciously abide in Him we have the liberty, not a liberty to our old nature or our self-will, but the Divine liberty from all self-will, to ask what we will, in the power of the new nature, and it shall be done. Let us keep this place, and believe even now that our intercession is heard, and that the Spirit of Supplication will be given all around us.

### THIRTIETH DAY

### WHAT TO PRAY—*For the Holy Spirit with the Word of God*

"Our gospel came not unto you in word only, but also in power, and in the Holy Ghost, and in much assurance."—1 Thess. 1:5.

"Those who preached unto you the gospel with the Holy Ghost sent forth from heaven."—1 Pet. 1:12.

What numbers of Bibles are being circulated. What numbers of sermons on the Bible are being preached. What numbers of Bibles are being read in home and school. How little blessing when it comes "in word" only; what Divine blessing and power when it comes "in the Holy Ghost," when it is preached "with the Holy Ghost sent forth from heaven." Pray for Bible circulation, and preaching and teaching and reading, that it may all be in the Holy Ghost, with much prayer. Pray for the power of the Spirit with the word in your own neighbourhood, wherever it is being read or heard. Let every mention of "The Word of God" waken intercession.

### HOW TO PRAY—*Watching and Praying*

"Continue steadfastly in prayer, watching therein with thanksgiving; withal praying for us also, that God may open for us a door for the word."—Col. 4:2, 3.

Do you not see how all depends upon God and prayer? As long as He lives and loves, and hears and works, as long as there are souls with hearts closed to the word, as long as there is work to be done in carrying the word—Pray without ceasing. Continue steadfastly in prayer, watching therein with thanksgiving. These words are for every Christian.

### THIRTY-FIRST DAY

### WHAT TO PRAY—*For the Spirit of Christ in His People*

"I am the Vine, ye are the branches."—John 15:5.
"That ye should do as I have done to you."—John 13:15.
As branches we are to be so like the Vine, so entirely identified with it, that all may see that we have the same nature, and life, and spirit. When we pray for the Spirit, let us not only think of a Spirit of power, but the very disposition and temper of Christ Jesus. Ask and expect nothing less: for yourself, and all God's children, cry for it.

### HOW TO PRAY—*Striving in Prayer*

"That ye strive together with me in your prayers to God for me."—Rom. 15:30.
"I would ye knew what great conflict I have for you."—Col. 2:1.
All the powers of evil seek to hinder us in prayer. Prayer is a conflict with opposing forces. It needs the whole heart and all our strength. May God give us grace to strive in prayer till we prevail.